RESEARCH ON SCHOOL RESTRUCTURING

Arthur K. Ellis and Jeffrey T. Fouts

EYE ON EDUCATION

EYE ON EDUCATION
P.O. BOX 388
PRINCETON JUNCTION, N.J. 08550
(609) 799-9188
(609) 799-3698 fax

The authors would like to acknowledge the work of Mary Novello, Jean Eisele, Rona Cornell, Juli Hynden, Detra Markey, and Joan Spingelt who helped assemble the research for this book.

Editorial and production services provided by Richard H. Adin Freelance Editorial Services, 9 Orchard Drive, Gardiner, NY 12515 (914-883-5884)

For information about permission to reproduce selections from this book, write: Eye On Education, Permissions Dept., P.O. Box 388, Princeton Junction, NJ 08550

ISBN 1-883001-09-9

Library of Congress Cataloging-in-Publication Data

Ellis, Arthur K.
    Research on school restructuring / Arthur K. Ellis and Jeffrey T. Fouts
        p.   cm.
    Includes bibliographical references.
    ISBN 1-883001-09-9
    1. Education—United States. 2. . Public Schools—United States 3. Educational change—United States   I. Fouts, Jeffrey T. II. Title.
LA217.2.E53 1994
370'.973—dc20   94-17750
                                                   CIP

Also from Eye On Education:

THE LIBRARY OF INNOVATIONS

Innovations in Parent and Family Involvement
by William Rioux and Nancy Berla

The Directory of Innovations in High Schools
by Gloria Frazier and Robert Sickles

Research on Educational Innovations
by Arthur Ellis and Jeffrey Fouts

THE LEADERSHIP AND MANAGEMENT SERIES

The Principal's Edge
by Jack McCall

The Administrator's Guide to Personal Productivity with the Time Management Checklist
by Harold Taylor

Quality and Education: Critical Linkages
by Betty L. McCormick

Transforming Education Through Total Quality Management: A Practitioner's Guide
by Franklin P. Schargel

Eye On Education welcomes your comments and inquiries about current and forthcoming publications. Please contact us at:

Eye On Education
P.O. Box 388
Princeton Junction, New Jersey 08550
(609) 799-9188 phone
(609) 799-3698 fax

ABOUT THE AUTHORS

Arthur K. Ellis is Professor of Education at Seattle Pacific University. Previously, he taught in public schools and at the University of Minnesota. He is the author of nine published books and numerous journal articles. He consults to numerous government agencies and to various school systems in the United States and abroad.

Jeffrey T. Fouts is Professor of Education at Seattle Pacific University. Previously, he taught in public schools in the State of Oregon. He is the author of three published books and has done research on classroom environments as well as consulting work in the United States and in other countries.

TABLE OF CONTENTS

PREFACE xi
   WHAT THIS BOOK IS AND IS NOT xiv

I THE NATURE OF RESTRUCTURING 1
   THE NEED FOR REFORM 5
   FROM REFORM TO RESTRUCTURING 6
   RESTRUCTURING OR TINKERING? 7
   THE MEANING OF RESTRUCTURING 9
   CONCLUSIONS 12
   REFERENCES 12

2 THE PROCESS OF RESTRUCTURING 13
   HOW INNOVATIONS MATERIALIZE 16
   THE SEARCH FOR PATTERNS 17
   CHAOS THEORY 18
   CONCLUSION 21
   REFERENCE 22

3 A MODEL OF RESTRUCTURING EFFORTS 23
   CLEAR THINKING ABOUT RESTRUCTURING 25
   GOAL-DRIVEN/PARTICIPATORY VS. ARBITRARY/MANDATED
      RESTRUCTURING 27
      GOAL-DRIVEN/PARTICIPATORY RESTRUCTURING 27
      ARBITRARY/MANDATED RESTRUCTURING 30
   CASE STUDIES 31

BUREAUCRATIC/CENTRALIZED VS.
    AUTHENTIC/FUNDAMENTAL RESTRUCTURING 33
    BUREAUCRATIC/CENTRALIZED RESTRUCTURING 33
    AUTHENTIC/FUNDAMENTAL RESTRUCTURING 34
    CASE STUDIES 35
    REFERENCE 37

4 EDUCATIONAL RESEARCH AND RESTRUCTURING 39
    "THE RESEARCH SAYS . . ." 42
    WHAT "KIND" OF RESEARCH? 43
    "IT PAYS TO BE IGNORANT" (OR DOES IT?) 47
    USING EDUCATIONAL RESEARCH 48
    THE FOLLOWING CHAPTERS 51
    REFERENCES 51

5 OUTCOME-BASED EDUCATION 51
    WHAT IS OUTCOME-BASED EDUCATION? 53
    A PRESCRIPTION FOR SCHOOL MALADIES 54
    REVERSING THE ORDER OF THINGS 56
    UNDERLYING PRINCIPLES 58
    TRADITIONAL, TRANSITIONAL, TRANSFORMATIONAL
       OBE 59
    IMPLEMENTING OBE 60
    EVALUATING OBE 61
    POTENTIAL AND PITFALLS 61
    THE RESEARCH BASE FOR OBE 63
    A RESEARCH AGENDA FOR OBE 64
    REFERENCES 65

6 SITE-BASED MANAGEMENT 67
    WHAT IS SITE-BASED MANAGEMENT? 69
    KEY ELEMENTS 72
    KEY QUESTIONS 73
    ADVICE FOR IMPLEMENTATION 73
    EVALUATING SITE BASED MANAGEMENT 74
    POTENTIAL AND PITFALLS 74
    THE RESEARCH BASE FOR SITE-BASED
       MANAGEMENT 77
    A RESEARCH AGENDA FOR SITE-BASED
       MANAGEMENT 81

REFERENCES 81

7 TOTAL QUALITY MANAGEMENT 83
  WHAT IS TOTAL QUALITY MANAGEMENT? 85
    TQM VS. OBE 90
    CRITICISMS AND WITTICISMS 91
  EVALUATING TOTAL QUALITY MANAGEMENT 92
    POTENTIAL AND PITFALLS 92
    THE RESEARCH BASE FOR TQM 94
    A RESEARCH AGENDA FOR TOTAL QUALITY
    MANAGEMENT 96
  REFERENCES 97

8 YEAR-ROUND SCHOOLS 99
  WHAT ARE YEAR-ROUND SCHOOLS? 101
    THE CONCERN WITH ECONOMY 101
    THE CONCERN WITH LEARNING 102
  EVALUATING YEAR-ROUND EDUCATION 105
    POTENTIAL AND PITFALLS 105
    EDUCATIONAL RESEARCH AND YEAR-ROUND
    EDUCATION 107
    A RESEARCH AGENDA FOR YEAR-ROUND
    EDUCATION 107
  REFERENCES 108

9 PARENTAL INVOLVEMENT 111
  WHAT IS PARENT INVOLVEMENT 113
  EVALUATING PARENTAL INVOLVEMENT 121
    POTENTIAL AND PITFALLS 121
    EDUCATIONAL RESEARCH ON PARENTAL
    INVOLVEMENT 123
  REFERENCES 125

10 EDUCATIONAL CHOICE 127
  WHAT IS EDUCATIONAL CHOICE? 129
    THE BIG DEBATE 132
  EVALUATING EDUCATIONAL CHOICE 140
    POTENTIAL AND PITFALLS 140
    EDUCATIONAL RESEARCH AND CHOICE 142
  REFERENCES 144

11 INSTRUCTIONAL GROUPING ALTERNATIVES 147
   WHAT ARE INSTRUCTIONAL GROUPING
      ALTERNATIVES? 149
      INSTRUCTIONAL GROUPING ALTERNATIVES IN THE
         ELEMENTARY SCHOOL 149
      INSTRUCTIONAL GROUPING ALTERNATIVES IN THE
         SECONDARY SCHOOL 153
   EVALUATING INSTRUCTIONAL GROUPING
      ALTERNATIVES 153
      POTENTIAL AND PITFALLS 153
      EDUCATIONAL RESEARCH AND INSTRUCTIONAL
         GROUPING 156
      NONGRADED EDUCATION 156
      ABILITY GROUPING 158
      SECONDARY GROUPING PRACTICES 159
   REFERENCES 160

12 ALTERNATIVE ASSESSMENT 163
   WHAT IS ALTERNATIVE ASSESSMENT? 165
      WHAT DID YA GIT? 166
      AUTHENTIC ASSESSMENT 167
      ALTERNATIVE ASSESSMENT STRATEGIES 171
   EVALUATING ALTERNATIVE ASSESSMENT 174
      POTENTIAL AND PITFALLS 174
      EDUCATIONAL RESEARCH AND ALTERNATIVE
         ASSESSMENT 175
   REFERENCES 175

13 EDUCATIONAL TECHNOLOGY 177
   WHAT IS EDUCATIONAL TECHNOLOGY? 179
      PROMISES TO KEEP? 183
   EVALUATING EDUCATIONAL TECHNOLOGY 184
      POTENTIAL AND PITFALLS 184
      EDUCATIONAL TECHNOLOGY AND EDUCATIONAL
         RESEARCH 187
   REFERENCES 190

14 COOPERATIVE LEARNING 193
   WHAT IS COOPERATIVE LEARNING? 195
      COOPERATIVE LEARNING MODELS 197

EVALUATING COOPERATIVE LEARNING 200

POTENTIAL AND PITFALLS 200

THE RESEARCH BASE FOR COOPERATIVE LEARNING . . 201

A RESEARCH AGENDA FOR COOPERATIVE

LEARNING 204

REFERENCES 204

15 THE SEARCH FOR MEANINGFUL CHANGE 207

A WALK DOWN THE BOULEVARD OF BROKEN

DREAMS 211

NECESSARY STEPS 214

TOWARD A HUMAN SCALE 215

TOWARD CONTEXT AND CONNECTIONS 216

CONCLUSIONS 220

WHAT SHOULD WE DO? 222

REFERENCES 223

BIBLIOGRAPHY 227

INDEX 249

The revolt against the classical dissectors and drillmasters was justified. So was the new interest in experimental science. The revolt against liberal education was not justified. Neither was the belief that the method of experimental science could replace the methods of history, philosophy, and the arts. As is common in educational discussion, the public had confused names and things. The dissectors and drillmasters had no more to do with liberal education than the ordinary college of liberal arts has to do with those arts today. And the fact that a method obtains sensational results in one field is no guarantee that it will obtain any results whatever in another.

Mortimer J. Adler
The Great Conversation Revisited

PREFACE

Unlike Alice in *Alice in Wonderland*, who always seems uncertain about who she is and where she is going, Dorothy in *The Wizard of Oz* forges ahead with unflagging confidence.

William Leach
Land of Desire

It is, of course, impossible to describe or even to list here all the changes . . . that have been introduced in the schools in response to the reformers' demands.

I.N. Thut, 1965

Welcome to this book. It is about school restructuring and the search for evidence in support of the many and varied attempts to change school life for the better. In some instances, our search for evidence was productive, in others, perhaps less so, but more about all that in due course.

In order to restructure anything, one must begin with the premise that there is an existing structure. Indeed there is. The structure of the schools as you and we know it is just over 100 years old. From the 1890s forward, schools have remained the same more than they have become different. In the early 1890s, the National Education Association (NEA) supported two elaborate commissions whose task it was, differentially, to give structure in the form of elements of standardization to American elementary and secondary schools.

So we have this structure called public schools, a complex system which includes a holding company of such diverse factors as grade levels, master schedules, school calendars, report cards, Carnegie units, diplomas, standardized tests, certified teachers and administrators, compulsory attendance, management techniques, lunch programs, and a host of other pieces, not to mention such incidentals as curriculum and instruction. Although it has been modified (some would say tinkered with) many times over the past century, all the changes have been new editions rather than original works.

Much of the battle for the school has been waged not strategically but tactically. By that we mean the deep structure has remained largely intact, and the attempts to reform the schools have themselves been an acknowledgment of its necessity. But there has been seemingly no end (with none in sight) to the tactical battles. To fold the combatants into two large camps misses much of the subtlety, but we'll do it anyway, staking our claim that the battle for the school is between traditionalists and progressives.

Traditionalists want to maintain or regain the sense of order, continuity, and simplicity of school offerings and basic purpose. Schools need to offer the essential knowledge, skills, and values that will be required of future citizens. They view the school as that one place where all the children have to come, and so the program must also address some of the deficits that families, church, social groups, and the community itself have, by default, created. Traditionalists are realists in the sense that they are willing to make necessary modifications along the way to improving life in schools.

Progressives are known more often than not for what they do not like, and in the case of schools what they do not like is the status quo. They feel that our school system, which they claim is based on a factory model, simply does not meet the needs of children. On the other hand, they don't really wish to tear it down, they just want to make it more child-centered, responsive, and relevant. If traditionalists are concerned with the products of our schools, progressives are concerned with the process of education. In some cases it's as concrete as the difference in philosophy between Outcome-Based Education and Total-Quality Education.

Those who would change the deep structure of American public education are found well beyond the left and right of center. They range from the deschoolers to the home schoolers. Their very intriguing perspectives are found on the margins of the debate. Even they recognize that if schools were closed tomorrow we would still have to find places to put most of the children.

WHAT THIS BOOK IS AND IS NOT

This is not a book of formulas for changing education. The pages are filled with descriptions and analyses of quite a few programs and models, but we are not in the business of promoting or denying support to any of them. That is a function of the evidence we gathered. This is not a book of organizational theories or organizational changes. This is not a book about leadership styles or principles of effective leadership. This is not a book that tells you what to do, but it may help you make some of your own decisions about that.

This is a book about why changes are needed and what those changes might be. It is a book about the major players in the restructuring movement. It is a book that focuses the arguments, such as they are, on the research base, the philosophical world view, and the elements of implementation for various proposed routes of restructuring.

We have proceeded on the assumption that our educational system needs help. We assume that you agree. Further, it is our assumption that all of us who care want to make good decisions because our individual children and their shared future are at stake. It is in this spirit that we write.

Arthur K. Ellis
Jeffrey T. Fouts

1

THE NATURE OF RESTRUCTURING

structure (noun): the interdependent parts in a particular pattern of organization.

restructure (verb): to effect a different configuration of the interdependent parts in a particular pattern of organization.

tinker (verb): to repair or adjust something in an unskillful manner.

In his report to the annual convention of the National Education Association, William Bagley, professor of education at Teachers College, Columbia University, noted several pressing problems with American public education. Among the problems Bagley cited were:

1. American elementary and secondary students fail to meet the standards of achievement attained by students in other countries.
2. An increasing number of high school students are basically illiterate.
3. Notable deficiencies exist in mathematics and grammar throughout the grade levels.
4. More money is being spent on education than ever before, but such problems as the crime rate continue to increase.

These comments come as no surprise either to professionals or the public. We've heard this before. However, Bagley's gloomy scenario was delivered not in the closing years of the 20th Century but in 1938. The French proverb, "the more things change, the more they remain the same," comes to mind.

One searches the pages of American school history looking

for a time of widespread satisfaction. It can't be found. Horace Mann himself spent the years from 1837 to 1848 writing 12 annual reports in which he attempted to structure and restructure American public education. This, of course, is small comfort at best to the beleaguered school superintendents, principals, and teachers attempting to defend the system against increasingly focused attacks. The fact is that even those who find themselves in such defensive positions fighting rear guard actions are themselves dissatisfied with the way things are.

Much of the discontent comes from the nature of schooling itself. This is so for three reasons. First, schooling is an organic concept and it, therefore, is ever changing. You can't compare schooling to a piece of architecture that, once it is completed, is something you like or don't like, but at least we know what it is (a cathedral, skyscraper, etc.). Schooling exists all around us in a multitude of continually changing forms. We judge it on the basis of certain "outcomes," such as test scores, dumbed-down textbooks, or number of teenage pregnancies, but what really are we judging? Mostly, our reactions are visceral and intuitive.

The second reason why schooling never seems to measure up to our expectations is that schools by nature are conservative, while society, at least in America, is dynamic, ever changing and moving forward. If we could change schools instantly to match the needs of America in the 1990s, society would still move forward leaving the schools behind. Consequently, schools are forever playing catch-up, chasing the carrot on the stick which is always in front of it.

The third reason is that each of us has an idealized sense, however incompletely formed, of what schools ought to be. Maybe that expectation comes from hazy recollections of childhood and a simpler time and place. Maybe it comes from a three-page distillation in some magazine where an author extols the virtues of Asian schools, especially their test scores. Or maybe it comes from having one's own child in a particularly disappointing classroom or school. The list goes on, but its common property is the measure of what we consider reality taken against something that could be much better than it is.

The point of this is not to excuse the many shortcomings of American public education. They are rather evident. The point is that a certain amount of dissatisfaction is inevitable. It will always be there, and to some extent it is a healthy thing. But what happens when the feelings of dissatisfaction rise to the point where widespread public support can no longer be taken for granted? That is exactly where we are today, and that fact alone separates the 1938 report mentioned earlier from the present situation.

But if it's true that misery loves company, then perhaps we can take some solace from the worldwide sense of discontent, not merely with school, but with institutions in general. Take a moment to consider the feeling of citizens toward government, the legal profession, and print and television journalism, just to name a few examples. And as educational consultants in Russia and China, we can tell you that the feelings of discontent with the way things are in the schools of those two great nations is quite widespread.

THE NEED FOR REFORM

Educational reform represents an attempt to redefine and reconfigure an entity (the public schools) that is complex, conservative, and bureaucratic by nature in order to meet the changes occurring in an often otherwise dynamic society. This is not an easy task. The rate of change in the various sectors of American society today and throughout much of the world is staggering. In the computer industry, for example, it is estimated that the entire knowledge base changes every 18 months. This is not to say that the public schools are a completely static entity, but as we examine the nature of the changes that they do make, we have questions about how substantive many of them are.

A static society is well-served by conservative and bureaucratic educational institutions. The educational establishment of China went unchanged for centuries because China's Confucian society was relatively static and stable. The educational system was the perfect place of incubation for the unchanging, predictable society for which it prepared bookkeepers, census takers, and the legions of other petty officials who kept the country running on a day-to-day basis. Japan and India, too, were, for centuries, stable, unchanging societies. But the serious intrusion of the West into these cultures in the 19th Century introduced dynamics that left the educational systems obsolete in a relatively short period of time. Even today, the Chinese are trying to bring about changes in their educational system—changes that will prove effective as this giant nation develops a market economy.

Russia today is attempting to deal with the aftermath of a Marxist/Leninist system that was in place for most of the 20th Century, shaping the country's schools in a totalitarian image. Now, with market forces loose in Russia and in many of the former Soviet republics, a completely new dynamic prevails. How the schools will adjust to such a cataclysmic upheaval is uncertain at best. The old infrastructure has collapsed, and the shape of things to come, whether curricular, organizational, or managerial is largely indeterminate.

In our country the alarm bells have been sounding for some time. In 1983, the famous *A Nation at Risk* report called for sweeping reform in the nation's schools. Also in 1983, John Goodlad's important book, *A Place Called School,* furnished its widespread readership with a clear and graphic description of the nature of curriculum and teaching in American schools. Goodlad pointed to the many shortcomings of our school system, and he has spent much of the rest of his distinguished career attempting to offer meaningful solutions, among them smaller schools, increased parent participation, and curricular offerings that lead to lifelong learning. As useful as both these efforts were, they were attempts at reform. The term reform means to correct or remove faults, indicating some things that canbe done while leaving the basic structure of schools in place.

FROM REFORM TO RESTRUCTURING

In the current debate, the term "reform" has been replaced with the term "restructuring." To restructure something (a term which the schools have borrowed from the business world, who in turn borrowed it from architecture) means to make fundamental changes in the pattern of the organization of the interdependent part of a system. Restructuring, in other words, calls for wholesale changes in the very fabric of the structure or in the very nature of the educational enterprise. For us to use such a term meaningfully implies that the old structure cannot be reformed, and it, therefore, must be replaced.

Perhaps an analogy from business, since the term came from that world anyway, serves a useful purpose. Many of the major business (commercial and industrial) firms in the United States are in the throes of restructuring efforts. General Motors, once the paradigm of what was right and good about American industry, and more recently the paradigm of what was wrong and shoddy about American industry, has gone through a fundamental restructuring phase. GM's old auto factories, and the methods used to run them, were so antiquated that it was determined that they could not be salvaged. A total shutdown of entire automobile plants, an extremely painful process at the human scale where jobs and families were at stake, was undertaken. New structures took their place, often in different states. The new structures were fundamentally different places from the old factories. They employed different machinery, often using robotics and other high technology tools. The relationship between management and labor was fundamentally reconsidered with an eye toward empowering workers. A host of new ideas from industrial psychology were employed. In some cases, even the car dealerships (Saturn, for example) were restructured to change the public's perception of the horrors involved in dickering on the price of a new car. The company has emerged from its restructuring efforts, shedding its image as a mortally wounded dinosaur, as a company with a future.

The implication for the schools is clear. The feeling that our schools are not working as well as they should be is too deep to ignore. So here we are in the age of restructuring.

RESTRUCTURING OR TINKERING?

There are no shortages of schools or school districts that are currently being restructured. At least the term "restructuring" is conspicuously attached to their efforts. The implication, one would imagine, is that something as fundamentally different as the educational equivalent of the new General Motors will emerge as a result. One hears about Outcome-Based Education,

Total Quality Education, School Choice, and other terms that give the impression of a complete rebuilding of the schools. We are convinced, however, that much of what is called restructuring brings to mind another term, one called "tinkering."

A tinker is an unskilled mender of broken things, a kind of fixit person. One dictionary definition, less kind, is that a tinker is an unskillful or clumsy worker, a bungler. To "tinker" means to work clumsily at something, to busy oneself frivolously with something. It's not a pretty picture that comes to mind; in fact, the assumption is that things will probably be worse as a result of the efforts brought to bear.

It becomes tinkering when new programs and protocols fail to address the underlying problems, philosophy, or basic assumptions that got us where we are in the first place. Innovations which do not qualitatively and fundamentally alter the nature of the enterprise hardly qualify as bona fide restructuring. They simply represent intrusions (however well-intentioned) into a complex system, and we should recognize them as that. It serves no long-term purpose to call such efforts restructuring, because where no changes are made in the deep structure of things no long-term benefits will be found. If you have been in this business for more than a year, you have some idea of what we are talking about. We advise those among our readership who are of more recent vintage to consult their history books.

Let's take a minute to examine some of the controlling factors of the current educational experience. They include, among others, an agrarian calendar; custodial/daycare responsibilities; textbook-driven curricula; seat time; Carnegie units; letter grades; standardized tests; teachers' unions; depersonalized environments; athletic teams; and alienated students. The factors noted here alone (and there are many more) are overwhelming. But naming them serially does not do justice to the situation. You must keep in mind that each of these factors *interacts* with all the others, creating a complex structure at every neighborhood school.

A school district that extends its calendar from 180 attendance days to 220 has not really restructured the school experience, only lengthened it. The likelihood is that what has happened is far closer to tinkering than to restructuring. A school district that focuses learning on outcomes rather than on goals has not restructured itself. It has merely made a tactical change in a complex system.

Imagine yourself standing at the edge of a woodland pond. Quiet and serene as it might appear, it is in fact a complex ecosystem, the home of all kinds of plants and animals living in symbiotic relationships. We know from experience that attempts to "improve" the pond are: (1) difficult; (2) apt to make things worse; and (3) raise the question, "what do we mean by improvement?" Setting aside the issue of making strategic changes, it's hard to resist the temptation to throw a stone into the still waters just to watch the ripples. The effect is rather impressive as concentric circles move quietly across the surface as a result of the initial splash. But the ripples are sure to fade and disappear just as so many of our reform attempts have done.

THE MEANING OF RESTRUCTURING

Beyond dictionary definitions, the meaning of restructuring grows increasingly complex. In recent times, some useful illustrative examples have emerged. Carl Glickman (1993, p. 88) has proposed that restructuring attempts should focus on three areas: (1) a vision of learning; (2) examples of restructuring of education at a level to achieve the vision; and (3) a coordinated plan at local, state, and national levels for inviting and assisting schools and districts to take choice, responsibility, and accountability for their own efforts. These three areas of concern are expanded in Figure 1.1. Glickman's model offers serious professionals a place to begin the process. Where the process takes them ought to be variable depending on local conditions and local dreams.

Another, more abbreviated, template for beginning the process of restructuring is that developed by the National Governors Association (NGA) (O'Neil, 1990). This group focuses on what they consider to be the four major components

---

FIGURE 1.1. COMPONENTS OF SCHOOL RESTRUCTURING

A Vision of Learning

    1. Learning should be an active process that demands full student participation in pedagogically valid work.

    2. Learning should be both an individual and cooperative venture.

    3. Learning should be goal oriented and connected to the real world.

    4. Learning should be personalized to allow students, together with their teachers to set learning goals.

    5. Learning should be documentable, diagnostic, and reflective, providing continuous feedback to students and parents.

    6. Learning should take place in a comfortable physical environment, and in an atmosphere of support and respect.

Examples of Restructuring of Education

    1. Grouping practices and promotion.

    2. Scheduling, grading and curriculum practices.

    3. Staffing practices.

    4. Textbooks, teaching materials, and technology.

    5. Assessment practices.

    6. School space and instructional time.

    7. Staff development and teacher evaluation.

A Coordinated Plan for Restructuring

    1. Give site-based flexibility with greater responsibility for willing schools that have the support of their district.

    2. Establish centers of educational innovation to assist schools in developing their site-based initiatives.

    3. Target "risk capital" for schools with high percentages of economically disadvantaged students.

    4. Establish university-school preparation sites to prepare bright, intellectual, and culturally diverse persons as the teaching force.

Source: Glickman, C.D. (1993). Restructuring Policy for America's Schools. *NASSP Bulletin* (January, 1993), pp. 87–97.

of restructuring efforts: (1) curriculum and instruction; (2) authority and decisionmaking; (3) staff roles; and (4) accountability systems. The recommendations of the NGA appear in Figure 1.2.

FIGURE 1.2. AREAS OF RESTRUCTURING

◆ *Curriculum and instruction* must be modified to support higher-order thinking by all students. Use of instructional time needs to be more flexible, learning activities must be made more challenging and engaging, and student grouping practices should promote student interaction and cooperative efforts.

◆ *Authority and decisionmaking* should be decentralized so that the most educationally important decisions are made at the school site. Teachers, administrators and parents should set the basic direction of the school and determine strategies and organizational instructional arrangements needed to achieve them.

◆ *New staff roles* must be developed so that teachers may more readily work together to improve instruction and so that experienced and talented teachers can support beginning teachers, plan and develop new curriculums, or design and implement staff development. Greater use of paraprofessionals should be considered. Principals will need to provide the vision to help shape new school structures, lead talented teachers, and take risks in an environment that rewards performance rather than compliance.

◆ *Accountability systems* must clearly link rewards and incentives to student performance at the building level. Schools must have more discretion and authority to achieve results and then be held accountable for results. States must develop measures to assess valued outcomes of performance of individual schools and link rewards and sanctions to results.

Source: O'Neil, J. (1990). "Piecing Together the Restructuring Puzzle." Educational Leadership, 47(7), p. 6.

CONCLUSIONS

The current widespread feelings of discontent over school practice and results have led to the cry for school restructuring. The term itself has emerged as a catchall for a variety of reform efforts in schools. Those efforts include a grab bag of innovations such as teacher empowerment, site-based decisionmaking, curriculum realignment, school choice, outcome-based education, community and/or parental involvement, and others.

Serious restructuring represents an attempt to get at the very essence of American education with an eye toward fundamental change. We suggest in this chapter that the public schools are (1) bureaucratic and resistant to fundamental change by their very nature and (2) too complex to be meaningfully changed by add-on treatments and serial, out-of-context innovations which underestimate the intricacies of school life.

REFERENCES

Glickman, C.D. (1993). Restructuring Policy for America's Schools. *NASSP Bulletin* (January, 1993), 87–97.

Goodlad, J.I. (1984). *A Place Called School: Prospects for the Future.* New York: McGraw-Hill.

O'Neil, J. (1990). Piecing Together the Restructuring Puzzle. *Educational Leadership,* 47(7).

United States Department of Education (1983). *A Nation At Risk: The Imperative for Educational Reform.* Washington, DC.

2

THE PROCESS OF RESTRUCTURING

Schools must be overhauled in ways that fundamentally change the institution of schooling itself.

John O'Neil

A struggle over how to manage schools over the next decades is under way. The outcome of that struggle will determine whether teachers are talented, responsible professionals or low-level closely managed bureaucrats.

Arthur Wise

It is hard to recall a time when school improvement of some sort wasn't on the educational agenda. Experienced teachers and administrators take for granted that each year brings one or more new trends to be implemented. It's a little like eating at a Chinese banquet where you aren't exactly sure just how many courses will be served in serial fashion. Just about the time your plate seems full, some new dish appears. A person could get indigestion. Each innovation is heralded with great fanfare. Promoters rave ecstatically about its merits. Staff developers and workshop impresarios gear up to educate the uninitiated. Quite often the workshop leaders are the same people who were enthusiastically touting something else a year or two ago. Maybe the innovation is the New Science or the New Math of the 1960s. Maybe it is Values Clarification or Career Education and we're in the 1970s. Maybe it is Mastery Learning or Refusal Skills and the decade is that of the 1980s. Or maybe we're closing in on the 21st Century and the topic is Total Quality Education or Outcome-Based Education, whatever they are.

The topics change, new ones emerge (what became of the last one, the one we tried last year?), and the only thing we feel sure about is that new ones will come along next year. The more paranoid have visions of some conspiratorial group meeting in secret, even as you read this, conjuring up next year's fad.

HOW INNOVATIONS MATERIALIZE

Actually, there is little evidence of conspiratorial plotting. Still, the paranoid aren't far off in some respects. Here is how it appears to work. Someone or some group builds a kind of model of teaching, learning, management, or organization. Maybe they got a grant, who knows? Generally the model is based on something occurring in learning theory, the business world, or perhaps it is merely rooted in some generalized dissatisfaction with the status quo. Often the theoretical construct, when there is one, is well-established. It may represent a refreshing set of new insights when applied to our field of education. This is certainly the case when it comes to the energizing intellectual/social ideas which are the basis of cooperative learning, one of the genuinely legitimate innovations of recent years. Theories of socially-constructed knowledge have been around since at least the 1930s, and when David and Roger Johnson, Robert Slavin, Shlomo Sharan, and others began to see the possibilities for school settings, cooperative learning was taken to the school-based application level. Often, however, educational innovations have very little to recommend them beyond the fever pitch and enthusiasm they generate in the hearts of the true believers.

Once a model is defined and written about by researchers and other theoreticians, events begin to take on a life of their own. Of course, the theory builders themselves generally continue to refine their ideas on the basis of further research. And applied research, including data gathering in school settings, begins as well, or at least it should. There are instances where this stage is skipped because, as one state department educator/bureaucrat recently noted, speaking about the idea of inclusion of special needs students in regular classroom settings, "there isn't time to wait around for the research because the needs are too great out there." No one can deny that the needs are great out there, but such logic has led us all down the garden path more than once.

THE SEARCH FOR PATTERNS

As confusing as all this change appears to be on the surface, there are some patterns. On closer inspection they become obvious. Let's look at them. One of the patterns has to do with change itself. In times past little change was noted from one generation to the next. In the Middle Ages, artisans and guild members might work on the same cathedral for generations. Sons took their fathers' places as masons, carpenters, joiners, etc., and in turn were replaced by their sons. Women did what their mothers had done before them. But the work was the same; the expectations were the same. Not only were innovations few and far between, but skills known in Ancient times had in some cases actually deteriorated and were lost. Therefore, there was no pervasive sense of the promise of change as progress.

This is no longer the case. In recent times, the pace of change has accelerated to the point that it has become dizzying. We have come to expect change as a natural occurrence. We would be surprised if it did not occur. Alvin Toffler (1970) called it "future shock," too much change in too short a time. New models of cars, running shoes, audio equipment, video games, etc., appear all the time. When something doesn't change, we wonder why.

Change is deeply imbedded in our world view, and we have come to equate it with progress. Changes in technology usually are just that: progress. New computers, for example, are miracle machines compared to their predecessors of just a few years ago. So by analogy, it is easy to assume that change equals progress. But it isn't that simple for at least two reasons: (1) technological change is qualitatively different from social change; and (2) what is, or appears to be, a positive change in and of itself may have rather complicated repercussions, some of which surface considerably after the change is implemented.

To take up the first point, that technological change is not the same as social change, it is well to bear in mind that schools and classrooms are socially-constructed environments. They cannot be equated with laboratory environments nor with natural-world environments. They have, and should have, all the qualities of our humanity: kindness, unpredictability, stubbornness, curiosity, differences, etc. This is what makes them ultimately worthwhile. It may have been lost in the mists of memory, but that's why you went into this profession in the first place. You wanted to make a difference in children's lives. You wanted to be a part of their growing up. You probably still do.

The changes that occur in socially-constructed environments such as schools are often more like the changes that occur in the world of fashion, not changes in the sense of progress as it occurs in technology. They often tend to be change for the sake of change, a kind of way of trying to make us think that improvements are really being made when it is questionable whether they are or not. So, if a notebook computer has more memory capacity than its predecessor, we can say that this represents a substantive change. On the other hand, if hemlines go up or down from one year to the next, that is not a substantive change.

The second point is equally elusive. Any change has a multitude of effects. For example, damming rivers is something we've gotten pretty good at. The short-term effects appear quite beneficial: flood control, irrigation, hydroelectricity, and so on. But the long-term effects may be mixed: reservoirs fill with silt, irrigated soil becomes brackish over time, and people living on the flood plain learn the hard way that rivers will go on periodic rampages in spite of our efforts to control them. This is not an attempt on our part to rant and rave against technological innovation. We merely wish to suggest that any attempt to alter a system will bring with it a host of unforeseen changes which we may or may not welcome. We wish to note as well that attempts to change, and hence "improve," school environments, with all their inherent complexities, are rather problematic. This is why most educational innovations are doomed to failure: a single innovation placed into the labyrinthine matrix of school life carries with it elements of the absurd, no matter how great it looks out of context.

CHAOS THEORY

The book (and film) *Jurassic Park*, by Michael Crichton, was the story of a "successful" attempt to clone dinosaur DNA, making it possible to bring prehistoric creatures to life in modern times. Taken out of any context and considered in a vacuum, the experiment "worked" wonderfully well. But, of course, there is always a context to anything we do. Even laboratory conditions represent a certain kind of context. As the story unfolded it became increasingly clear that a host of untoward, unanticipated complexities were emerging. The "system" into which the dinosaurs were placed, in this case an island off the coast of Central America, was more chaotic than the genetic engineers who masterminded the plan had figured it would be. But it was chaotic simply because it *was* a natural environment with all the typical accompanying complexities. Events quickly spun out of control creating the horrors that readers and movie goers had hoped for.

Chaos theory comes from the natural sciences. Chaos is to be found somewhere between completely controlled and completely random conditions. In other words, in spite of the unordered image it conveys, chaos is quite normal. A completely ordered environment is probably only theoretically possible, but it can be approximated under laboratory conditions, for example, in a wind tunnel used for testing new aircraft, or in an advertisement showing someone with perfectly gorgeous hair. The whole theory of advertising and consumer consumption is based on the idea of presenting to the would-be consumer a perfectly ordered, idealized image of a product or service.

On the other hand, random environments are just as hard to come by, maybe more so. In a random environment, *nothing* works according to any plan—stuff, as they say, just happens. The tea party hosted by the Mad Hatter and the March Hare in *Alice in Wonderland* comes to mind. In a random, or haphazard, environment prediction breaks down. Nothing works according to any discernible goal structure or plan. It becomes impossible to make plans, to follow through on things, or even to figure out what is going on. That appeared to be the goal (the creation of a seemingly random environment) of the archfiend, The Joker, in the film "Batman."

A school and the classrooms found within a school ought to be case studies in chaos. This is to say that at their best they should represent something between ordered and random

environments. The recent escalation of violent activity in school
settings gives rise to the specter of randomness. When teachers
and students must fear for their very safety in an environment
which is ostensibly about learning, it becomes impossible to
concentrate on academics. But in spite of increased violence and
the threat it poses to education, far more schools are found
toward the ordered end of the spectrum than toward the
random end. It is in our attempts to order school environments
beyond a degree conducive to true learning that students and
teachers fail to discover themselves as productive citizens in a
democratic society. This is so because such highly ordered
environments are too syntactically simple to allow intellectual,
moral, and social growth to emerge in any coherent fashion.

This brings us to an examination of the structure of
classroom and school environments. Perhaps you noticed that
when a student teacher, a beginner, is given a class to teach the
primary issue seems to be discipline or the beginner's ability to
manage the class successfully. So important is this matter that
it takes precedence, in the minds of all concerned, over the
student teacher's grasp of the material to be taught. And it is
certainly rated above such accompanying matters as how much
the student teacher cares for the students, how much he or she
loves the subject matter, or how imaginative and creative he or
she is. The management factor is so paramount that even the
subject matter to be taught is woven into the texture of control.
This is accomplished through an expectation common among
supervisors: that the student teacher will prepare an elaborate
lesson plan. Invariably the expected lesson plan is a guide for
the preplanned, orchestrated flow of instruction. In other
words, the idea of a lesson plan is that it enables a teacher to
control and predict events. This sense of propriety visited upon
the student teacher carries over to the professional level; it
doesn't go away. Control, more than any other single concept,
is a predominant goal in the structure of public education.

Those who are truly serious about restructuring education
might well begin here because the lesson plan with its
prefabricated sense of teaching and learning serves as a telling
metaphor for much of what is wrong in the present system. Of
course, the dominant role of textbooks as the de facto
curriculum in American public education would serve just as

well to make the case. In a nutshell, what is wrong is that school has become a place primarily devoted to management, not to learning. And because this is so, attempts to restructure school environments through Site-Based Management, Outcome-Based Education, and even through such well-researched approaches as Cooperative Learning, are highly problematic and bound to result in disappointment.

The perceived randomness of school environments is not that at all. They are in fact primarily places devoted to order. It is when they are not orderly that people take notice and that condemnation is visited on the schools. But at the same time that it expects order, the public also demands better test scores. It is not clear exactly what the public demand is in this regard. Since test scores have declined with some regularity over the past two decades, it may be only that the public wishes to stop the downslide. No doubt they would appreciate it if scores were to increase every year, but such an expectation seems unreasonable in light of the array of sociological factors about which only the most naive citizens are unaware. Attempts to restructure school environments without serious attention to the more fundamental issue of home and community environments will be largely unsuccessful because home and community are built more deeply into the fabric of life than are the schools.

CONCLUSION

Attempts to restructure classrooms and schools are generally tied somehow to a vision of improved environments for learning and therefore improved consumer satisfaction, and, ultimately, higher test scores. The word consumer is obviously a business term, and we use it here as a metaphor. Examples of consumers in education are students, teachers, administrators, parents, and others who have a vested interested in the life and productivity of our schools. As we examine the array of restructuring efforts currently underway in the schools, it will be well for you to bear in mind the image of learning environments as chaotic but purposeful when they are at their best. The need to improve test scores lies always in the shadow of reform, imperceptible to some as a goal but always demanded by the public in the end.

The recent attempts to restructure American industry, especially the automobile, steel, and other durable goods sectors, illustrate to us how difficult and how humanly demanding such attempts truly are. Our nation's schools are no less complex, and the problems are every bit as deeply imbedded. The chapters which follow are designed to shed some light on various restructuring efforts. You must decide for yourself how serious, fundamental, and lasting these attempts will be. It is our hope that as you examine the many different approaches you will be able to make thoughtful decisions about how to sort out the differences between tinkering and true restructuring.

REFERENCE

Toffler, A. (1970). *Future Shock*. New York: Bantam Books.

3

A MODEL OF RESTRUCTURING EFFORTS

Words mean whatever I say they mean.

Humpty Dumpty

Change is one thing, progress is another.

Bertrand Russell

Do not repeat the tactics which have gained you one victory, but let your methods be regulated by the infinite variety of circumstances.

Sun Tzu

CLEAR THINKING ABOUT RESTRUCTURING

A concept like restructuring is so broad that it can mean virtually anything the user wants it to mean. Educators tend to use the term in a variety of ways, perhaps in an unwitting attempt to prove that Humpty Dumpty had sensed something profound. It has been used in the name of minor reforms or changes in schools, what a person might call tinkering with the system. On the other hand, it can signal a revolutionary set of changes for the entire educational system.

We think that it is important for all of us to refine our thinking about the term restructuring. To engage such a process we have chosen to relate it to several broad movements each of which represents an attempt to restructure education. The various movements differ considerably in scope and ambition. Some are more closely identified with curriculum and instruction, others with organization, and still others with locus of control. They are, in fact, a haphazard collection of trends, innovations, and insights. The main thing they have in common is a claim to making schools, and, therefore, education, better. As you might expect, some are more profound than others. As you also might expect, they represent often contradictory sets of purposes, but that has not stopped some groups from trying to paste together certain programs that we think will result in pedagogical crosscurrents at best and scholastic rip tides at worst. And finally, they become metaphors for our own wonderful democratic system considered at its idealized best with all its chaos and decentralized, entrepreneurial sense of eternal optimism that has led us more than once to think that maybe, just maybe, this is the answer we've been looking for all along.

To conduct our review of the topics that appear in these pages, we have constructed two sets of perspectives on restructuring. These constructs are somewhat arbitrary, but we hope they will furnish you with a reasonable vantage point for thinking about change in schools. The first set presents the *energizing forces* behind restructuring. We call this set of perspectives goal-driven/participatory restructuring vs. arbitrary/mandated restructuring (Fig. 3.1). The second set of per-

---

FIGURE 3.1. RESTRUCTURING

Goal-Driven/Participatory	*Arbitrary/Mandated*
Focused	Random
Theory based	Atheoretical
Internal needs	External demands
Inclusive	Forced
Organic	Top-down
Internal locus	External locus

---

spectives is about the *outcomes* of restructuring efforts. We call this bureaucratic/centralized restructuring vs. authentic/fundamental restructuring (Fig. 3.2).

FIGURE 3.2. RESTRUCTURING

Bureaucratic/Centralized	*Authentic/Fundamental*
School	**Education**
Time schedule	Learning
Calendar	Reality
Administration	Synergistic
Decisionmaking	Systemic
Particularistic	Localized
Add-ons	Holistic
Slogans	
Fads	

GOAL-DRIVEN/PARTICIPATORY VS. ARBITRARY/MANDATED RESTRUCTURING

GOAL-DRIVEN/PARTICIPATORY RESTRUCTURING

To be successful, restructuring must start with a few clear goals to be achieved. Clear goals do not ensure success because a lot can happen along the way, but without them it seems unlikely that a school or district will emerge from the process triumphantly. Anything less than a goal-driven process is probably akin to the rather familiar image of rearranging the deck chairs on the *Titanic*. Without clear believed-in goals, restructuring becomes change without purpose. In goal-driven restructuring, the identified purpose(s) of the educational experience defines the nature of the changes sought. It has been our experience as program evaluators that this seemingly obvious step is often lost in the swirling currents of educational change. We have stood helplessly by watching as schools initiated restructuring efforts, implemented a hodgepodge of programs and changes with no clear believed-in goal(s). It is not a pretty sight. Sooner or later someone (teachers, parents, the local media) will ask, "Why are we doing this?". It's a difficult question to answer, and it has the effect of eroding public confidence in the schools.

When the goals of education are clearly agreed upon by those who must live with them, the direction for restructuring becomes quite clear. Questions about what changes to make or what programs to implement are answered by the efficacy of those programs in relation to the educational goals. The menu of possible changes is narrowed and focused by the anticipated results. No changes are undertaken unless they are thought to clearly facilitate goal attainment. For example, if the goal of the reform effort is to increase student retention and graduation rates, restructuring efforts which include an alternative scheduling system for a high school involving weekend and evening classes combined with a more relational counseling approach might be chosen over some type of multiage grouping of students because it is thought to have a more direct impact on the goal. Similarly, the focus on educational technology may or may not take a back seat to the implementation of a foreign language curriculum if developing international perspectives is the educational goal.

This simple idea becomes confounded, more often than not, in the rush to innovation. On the happier side of the ledger it has been our pleasure to witness restructuring efforts which were successfully driven by a clear goal structure. In these situations, agreed-on changes were selected thoughtfully and deliberately rather than by the simple momentum to change. In these schools there are true "instructional leaders," people concerned with learning first, and with a clear sense of priorities. In such schools administrators, teachers, students, and parents *knew and agreed on the changes to be made.*

We offer you the following example from our very recent experience as program evaluators. A group of faculty and administrators at Kent-Meridian Senior High School, Kent, Washington, agreed on a restructuring goal to create a school-within-the-school. The school-within-the-school would focus on health-sciences in an interdisciplinary way and would represent an attempt to integrate a group of faculty and one-fourth of the student body. Notice that the focus was on the integration of *people* rather than merely on subject matter. The parents and their children who also liked the idea could sign up for the program. The first year program evaluation focused on the question of to what degree students in the health-science school were experiencing a *qualitatively different* educational experience, or true fundamental restructuring. Using an educational environmental assessment technique, the first year showed efficacious results in the sought-after areas of student involvement, affiliation, teacher support for students, and innovation in classroom activities. Other variables such as disciplinary referrals, absenteeism, and suspensions were clearly in favor of the school-within-the-school when compared to the regular program. These are not trivial matters in today's schools. The graph in Figure 3.3 illustrates some of the findings from the program evaluation research.

FIGURE 3.3. FINDINGS FROM THE PROGRAM EVALUATION RESEARCH

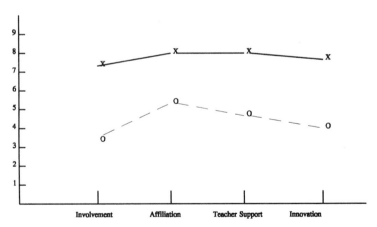

X scores represent the type of education experience of the students in the Health Science School.

0 scores represent the type of educational experience of the sutdents in the traditional program.

Clear goals are essential, but they are not sufficient of themselves. Dictators often have clear goals, but the goals may be neither agreed to nor understood by the people. We wish to suggest that a goal is not really meaningful until it is (1) understood and (2) agreed to by all who will be affected by its result. The German philosopher Jurgen Habermas (1974) wrote about his concept of the "validity of an idea." Habermas argued that an idea is not valid until everyone whom the idea might affect has had opportunity to agree to the idea. Therefore, if a school or district were to embark on a given restructuring venture, it would be incumbent on school leaders to *include* all those who will be affected by the idea in information, conversation, and debate to the point that the "stakeholders" agree it is something that needs to be done. This seems at first blush to be too cumbersome, time consuming, and unruly. In fact, it saves those involved from all kinds of untoward circumstances down the road. And equally significant, it is the democratic thing to do.

ARBITRARY/MANDATED RESTRUCTURING

We have talked on more than one occasion with school principals who tell us that they have been ordered to put together a restructuring plan for their school. Never mind if the job the school has done is good, bad, or indifferent. The word has come down from the top, and the expectation is there: all the schools in District X are to be restructured. The expectation may be to use outcome-based education. Perhaps the directive is to implement a whole-language curriculum, an interdisciplinary curriculum, or some other innovation. Directives from a top-down perspective and vague feelings of discontent take the place of a clear vision of what needs to be accomplished and why. All that is really understood is that change must be made. Lest you think we are building a straw man scenario here, need we remind you of the many arbitrarily enforced cure-alls in recent educational history including behavioral objectives, ITIP, state-mandated SLO's, competency-based education, etc.? Few of these were actually discussed and thoughtfully considered by local folks who then agreed that "this" is the way we should proceed. Rather they were all (and there have been many others) top-down protocols that purported to improve instruction and, by implication, raise test scores. But there is not evidence that it happened. Such arbitrary restructuring or tinkering may give an impression to some that innovation is taking place, but the more lasting outcome is cynicism.

CASE STUDIES

Let's examine two case studies in school reform. Brookside Elementary School and Northfield Elementary School are in fact composites of schools that demonstrate the differences between goal-driven and arbitrary restructuring.

Brookside and Northfield elementary schools might be described as "typical" suburban schools, each with a middle class student body. As part of a restructuring effort articulated by the school board, a degree of site-based management has been authorized at both schools. Each school is expected to identify "excellence" and to change in some reasonable way. At the root of site-based management is the question, "Once you have control at the local school level, what do you do with it?" Neither Brookside nor Northfield is doing a bad job of educating children; neither are they considered to be stellar schools in the district. Each school responded differently to its new-found decisionmaking authority.

Brookside has a principal and faculty who believe that the school could be a much better place than it is if it acts on a clear vision. After careful planning and consultation with administration, teachers, parents, and community groups, the school has identified three goals: (1) the development of a more child-centered environment; (2) an increase in student-to-student interaction; and (3) an increase in student knowledge and use of technologies.

With these clearly articulated and agreed-on goals, a search was made for useful information about new programs and models, including shared decisionmaking, site councils, cooperative learning, interdisciplinary curricula, and computer-based learning. With the full knowledge that many things could be done in the name of innovation, this school focused only on those that would directly support the achievement of its goals. Therefore, many of the current fads and trends were rejected, not because they are not sound practices, but because they did not facilitate the school's goal attainment. From all the available options the teachers chose the following:

(1) Development of a more child-centered environment—student learning centers, increased amount of free time, cooperative learning strategies, and a stronger emphasis on an integrated curriculum.

(2) An increase in student-to-student interaction—increased emphasis on group projects, cooperative learning, friendships, and thinking-aloud-with-partner strategies.

(3) Increased knowledge about technologies—computers in every classroom, writing programs, a technology student learning center, and student-created databases.

Because the goals were (1) few, (2) simple, (3) clear, and (4) agreed-on, the processes of monitoring, reflecting, evaluating, and measuring stood out in sharp relief as the school year progressed.

Northfield Elementary was given the same decisionmaking authority, but the results were rather different. Lacking vision, leadership, and a clear goal structure, the school didn't quite know what to do with its new found authority. The principal's response was a perusal of the horizon for what changes and innovations were being implemented in other schools, and selected several from the menu because they sounded good.

It was decided that all teachers would use cooperative learning in their classrooms. Whole language reading materials were purchased and were to be used in the new multiage reading groups that were to be implemented by the teachers. A number of teachers were strong advocates of portfolio assessment, so that also was added to the mix. None of the changes were necessarily bad ideas, but there were some teachers who were skeptical, responding among themselves with the comment, "here we go again." Some parents were less than pleased with what was going on, and a few raised questions in public causing problems for the teachers and principal. Other parents claimed they really didn't know much about what was going on, a sure danger sign in the annals of innovation. There was a perception of arbitrariness toward the changes. It was disquieting and discouraging to many involved.

Some restructuring is carefully and democratically planned, and some restructuring is haphazard and faddish. In schools like Northfield, those most affected by change were not given the opportunity to develop and implement a clear vision. In such schools, at some point into the changes, things have a tendency to revert back to their old ways. Inertia reasserts itself and regains control. In schools like Brookside, where teachers, administrators, students, and parents carefully articulate a set of meaningful goals, restructuring is much more likely to have a lasting effect.

BUREAUCRATIC/CENTRALIZED VS. AUTHENTIC/FUNDAMENTAL RESTRUCTURING

BUREAUCRATIC/CENTRALIZED RESTRUCTURING

We live in a time when it is expected that schools will do something in the area of educational restructuring. As a result, some schools make changes because they feel they have to just to "keep up." Such bureaucratic restructuring involves changed environments with the idea that somehow the learning environment will improve. There are no shortages of examples in this regard: a high school that shifts from a six period day to a seven period day while leaving the deep structure of things intact; a district that changes from 9-month to year-round school without making instructional/curricular changes; an elementary school that drops its traditional graded structure and adopts a nongraded approach but does not commit itself to a coherent philosophy of childhood growth and development. Bureaucratic changes are related to student learning only in an indirect sense; it has been our experience that they do not yield improved student learning in any lasting, significant sense. Site-based management, for example, is a bureaucratic maneuver that may have very little impact on the lives of students. Its impact on the lives of teachers and principals may, in fact, be negative if it represents change for the sake of staying current with the latest trends. Of course, like the other changes we just noted, it has the potential for changing the educational experience of students and teachers, but lasting improvement will not occur simply as a result of such changes. There must a context of purpose, meaning, and consensus.

AUTHENTIC/FUNDAMENTAL RESTRUCTURING

This type of restructuring represents change consciously chosen to bring about qualitatively different school experiences for teachers and students. These are the changes that flow from an examination of the very essence of education. A year-round calendar does not lead to qualitative change. However, an interdisciplinary curriculum program is based on an educational philosophy distinctly different from the typical segmented curriculum. It makes qualitatively different demands on teachers and students. When it is integrated with other approaches, such as cooperative learning, there is the potential for a fundamental difference in what and how students are asked to learn. But even here, the deeper question of "why" always remains to be answered. Why do we want to integrate the curriculum? Why do we want to have students learn cooperatively?

It might seem logical to assume that we are suggesting that authentic/fundamental restructuring can only occur when substantive issues such as curriculum and instruction are addressed. Further, you may be thinking that our opinion of organizational changes is such that we banish them to a world of outer darkness, considering them tinkering at best. Actually, both are necessary for meaningful change to occur. If, for example, we integrated the curriculum (substantive change), it might also make sense to adopt a nongraded approach (organizational change). By changing the organizational structure we make it far more possible to integrate students across age boundaries, and integrating students is really a requisite condition to a more fully integrated curriculum. This in turn builds a case for cooperative learning because working together demands certain interpersonal skills that cooperative learning offers.

CASE STUDIES

John Adams High School and Woodrow Wilson High School are composites of a number of schools we have worked with over the years. Both schools have been directed to restructure and have been given a degree of site-based authority. John Adams High School incorporated career-awareness preparation into its curriculum, placing juniors and seniors in community internships in various businesses and professions. Teachers integrated "real world" problems identified by the students during their internships into the course of study. Community resource people became involved in assisting in classes, interacting regularly with teachers and students. This application of the subject content to real-life situations required students to demonstrate a type of learning they had rarely, if ever, experienced. The school schedule was modified to include some evening and weekend classes, allowing the flexibility necessary to accommodate both internships and in-school learning.

These changes at John Adams High School resulted in an authentic, fundamental restructuring of the education the students were receiving. Their perceptions of the usefulness of the curriculum and the importance of school to their future professional success was altered. They were learning at a different level, applying knowledge to meaningful problems, a new experience for most. The changes were in fact the result of a philosophy of teaching and learning that had started with a few dedicated teachers, but which came to include administrators, students, parents, and community people. The curriculum did not look the same, the teaching changed, learning changed, even the school day changed. The changes were fundamental, inclusive of those who would be affected, and purposeful.

At Woodrow Wilson High School changes were also made. Block scheduling of classes was instituted. Block schedules allow teachers to have a class for 2–3 hours at a time during the day, for 2 or 3 days a week. It was also decided to adopt a year-round schedule following the 45–15 model (45 days on, 15 days off). Evening classes were added to the schedule in order to free students during the day so they could work at their jobs.

The changes at Woodrow Wilson High were qualitatively different from those made at John Adams. The changes made at Woodrow Wilson were primarily changes made in the bureaucratic structure of the school. They were top-down changes, emanating from centralized sources, and they were rationalized on the basis of an examination of trends in secondary education. The learning experiences didn't look much different from the way they looked before. Mainly they were different because they took place at different times of the day, week, or year. The students were asked to learn the same things.

The model of school restructuring shown in Figure 3.4, illustrates the importance of multiple forces at work. These forces are not always easily found on one end of these continua or the other. In fact, seldom are restructuring efforts as clear cut as we would like them to be. Still, it is helpful to think of restructuring efforts as falling into one of the four quadrants of the model. For example, some school restructuring is clearly goal oriented and participatory, resulting in changes that are fundamental in nature of the education process. Such restructuring would be the type that could be placed in Quadrant I. It is also possible that mandated or arbitrary forces for restructuring could result in fundamental changes (probably by chance). Such restructuring would fall in Quadrant II. Goal-oriented/participatory forces could lead to changes in the educational bureaucracy resulting in fundamental changes, but if those bureaucratic changes are largely ineffective, the restructuring effort would be in Quadrant III. Finally, changes in the bureaucracy that are arbitrary would fall in Quadrant IV.

FIGURE 3.4. A MODEL OF SCHOOL RESTRUCTURING

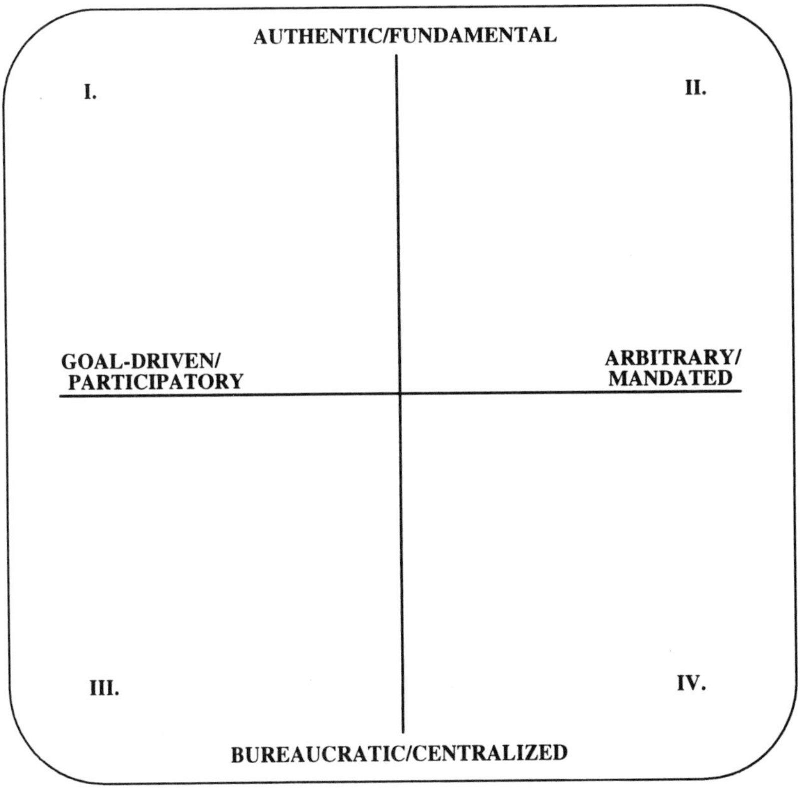

AUTHENTIC/FUNDAMENTAL

I.

II.

GOAL-DRIVEN/
PARTICIPATORY

ARBITRARY/
MANDATED

III.

IV.

BUREAUCRATIC/CENTRALIZED

We suggest that Quadrant I represents the most desirable sense of reform. In this quadrant are the changes that are most likely to be long lasting and meaningful. Quadrant IV changes are likely to be short-lived and will probably fail to bring any meaningful change to the lives of teachers and students. Worse yet, is the sense of cynicism fostered by such changes.

REFERENCE

Habermas, J. (1974). *Theory and Practice.* London: Heinemann Educational Books.

4

EDUCATIONAL RESEARCH AND RESTRUCTURING[1]

In research the horizon recedes as we advance, and is no nearer at sixty than it was at twenty. As the power of endurance weakens with age, the urgency of the pursuit grows more intense. . . . And research is always incomplete.

Mark Pattison

Educational research is simply scientific verification of the obvious.

Anonymous graduate research student

Clear goals are necessary and useful; but what happens along the way is what really matters.

Philo Santini

---

[1] Portions of this chapter appear in our earlier book, Research on Educational Innovations (1993). Used by Permission of the publisher, Eye on Education, Princeton Junction, NJ.

Restructuring efforts, all the rage currently, inevitably claim to be based on research findings. Why shouldn't they? The body of educational research has grown exponentially in quantity and quality in the past 20 years. Outstanding educational researchers such as Lee Schulman, Robert Slavin, Jerome Bruner, David Pearson, John Goodlad, Jere Brophy, Paula Short, Thomas Good, Nell Noddings, Benjamin Bloom, Herbert Walberg, David and Roger Johnson, and other notables, make up a veritable hall of fame in our field. Their insights to teaching and learning furnish administrators and teachers with an increasingly clear sense of the possibilities for improvement. One could argue that what we do is beginning to catch up with the two other cooperative arts, medicine and agriculture, in that at long last we have a guiding body of evidence to inform practice. Still, it isn't easy.

Any attempt by you to use research findings to support your restructuring efforts will encounter the ambiguities of applying research from somewhere else (no matter how good it was) to your local situation. This is so because no two socially-constructed situations are the same. Sometimes it is in the differences that the measure of success or failure is found. This is merely one of the problems, and it may not be the biggest. Ironically, the more successful a study is in its attempts to control factors affecting its internal and external validity, the less it will probably resemble your unique situation. This is not a reason to throw in the towel and give up. It is just our way of saying that you must be a student of your situation, reflecting thoughtfully on the needs and seeking advice from all those who will be affected by the changes to be made.

It is beyond the scope of this book to provide an in-depth analysis of the protocols of educational research. What we *have* attempted is to provide you with a framework by which you may discern the wide range of research claims that are made in the educational community. It is a model that we have articulated and used elsewhere (Ellis & Fouts, 1993) with some success. It is a simple model. We examine the published research base and resulting claims made in behalf of a number of educational innovations and programs. We'll show you how it works.

"The Research Says . . ."

Have you ever found yourself at a meeting or conference listening to a speaker who pauses dramatically and states in august tones, "well, the research says. . . ."? Everyone, including perhaps you yourself, quickly puts pen to paper in anticipation of some significant bombshell that will change school life for evermore. If only you or I had a nickel for every time an education hustler has used such a phrase! If only it were as significant a statement as it appears to be to the uninitiated. The only appropriate response that comes to mind in the midst of such confusion is, "What research?"

In fact the claim of virtually all innovators or purveyors of innovation is that research has in some strategic way played an important part in the evolution and development of their ideas, programs, or materials. And in some sense, the claim is generally true, but often misleading. For example, if someone claims his/her program for elementary children is based in part on learning transfer, we may be impressed. After all, the concept of transfer of learning is well-documented in the annals of psychological research. But the jump from research in a laboratory setting to classroom application is a long jump.

WHAT "KIND" OF RESEARCH?

We will show you a classification system that will prove helpful as you attempt to sort out the different kinds of research that is conducted. With this knowledge you will be able to determine for yourself what is behind the statement, "the research says. . . ."

In essence, there are three levels of research that have implications for educational innovation. The first is basic or pure research done in laboratory settings; the second is applied research done in school settings; and the third is evaluation research applied to school programs. Each is quite different from the others, and each yields is own unique types of conclusions as shown graphically in Figure 4.1.

Level 1 research is basic or pure research on learning and behavior. It is most commonly conducted in laboratory settings by psychologists, learning theorists, linguists, etc. Its purpose is to establish a theoretical construct or idea as having some validity. For example, Jean Piaget constructed a theory of stages of intellectual development through which children pass on their way to adult thought (Piaget, 1960). Jerome Bruner constructed a theory of the structure of knowledge which included alternative ways by which knowledge of some reality could be represented to learners (Bruner, 1966). Howard Gardner has constructed a theory of multiple intelligences (Gardner, 1986).

Although Level 1 research can serve as a foundation for curriculum development, it is not designed to answer applied educational questions. When Piaget claimed on the basis of his research that most 8-year-olds are in a stage of concrete operations, many builders of experimental curriculum packages decided to put together mathematics and science activities that involved manipulative materials. Rightly or wrongly, they did so on the assumption that the message from pure research could be applied to groups of 25 or 30 children learning together in a classroom setting. The extent to which it is reasonable to do this is really a function of Level 2 research.

Level 2 research involves studies the purpose of which are to determine the efficacy of particular programs or instructional methods, etc., in educational settings. Such studies are generally conducted by educational researchers who are interested in applying theories and procedures developed at the pure or basic level. For example, an educational researcher might attempt to setup controlled conditions in several classrooms for the purpose of comparingcooperative learning in social studies with independent student learning. The experimental conditions might call for randomly assigning students and teachers to dif-

---

FIGURE 4.1. THE THREE LEVELS OF EDUCATIONAL RESEARCH

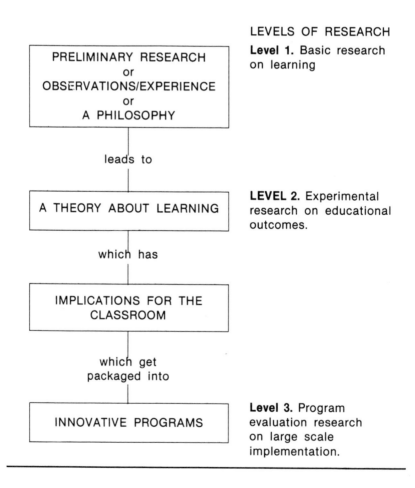

ferent treatment modes or conditions where the same material is studied. Pre- and post-tests may be administered to all participants and comparisons made to determine whether a statistically significant difference occurred between or among treatments.

Level 2 research is applied research because (1) it is conducted in the same or similar settings that are actually found in schools, and (2) it makes no attempt to develop a theory, but rather attempts to make instructional or curricular applications of a given theory. At its best, Level 2 research provides practical insights that cannot be derived directly from pure research. Thus, even though we all can agree that reinforcement has been shown to be a powerful psychological concept by pure researchers, it remains for the Level 2 researcher to demonstrate how it might be advantageous to apply reinforcement in teaching in classroom settings.

Level 2 research is crucial to the process of validation of programs or methods of instruction. But time and time again, this step is simply ignored or poorly crafted as program developers or purveyors tout their product. To return to the ITIP or PET "theory into practice" model for a moment, we can see in retrospect that it claimed its validity on the basis of such pure or basic research constructs as reinforcement, transfer, retention, etc., which are real enough. But it was almost totally lacking in any proof of what happens when you take those constructs and package them up for use by teachers in classroom settings. The same thing can be said for a number of other programs that have swept the country, e.g., "Assertive Discipline," "TESA," and higher level thinking strategies.

One of the best sources for school personnel to search at Level 2 is the journal, *Review of Educational Research*, which carries reviews and meta analyses of various programs, projects, and packages. If nothing else, it will give you insight into the sheer amount of applied research that has been conducted in a given area.

A final point about Level 2 research is that each study, even if it represents good research, is severely limited in its generalizability. If, for example, a study of teaching methods of reading and literature were conducted with 4th grade inner city children, then, whatever the results, it would be unwise to generalize them to rural 8th grade students. This is why large numbers of good investigations about a given program must be carried out before school districts jump on this or that bandwagon. Cooperative learning, in our opinion, has been investigated in such a wide variety of school-based settings that its Level 2 foundation is quite secure, especially compared to most other innovations.

Level 3 research is evaluation research designed to determine the efficacy of programs at the level of school or district implementation. It is by far the least likely of the three types to be carried out in any systematic way, and because of this programs (good, bad, or indifferent) usually just go away in time, replaced by the latest fad.

Examples of Level 3 research include evaluation studies that examine the overall effects on teachers and students of a particular district- or schoolwide innovation. If a district changes over from basal reading instruction to whole language learning, for example, it is the job of evaluation researchers to determine exactly what changes were brought about and what the results of those changes were. This might involve interviews with teachers, students, and parents, the application of classroom environmental scales to determine student perceptions of whole language learning, examinations of achievement data, and observations in classrooms to document exactly how the new program is being implemented.

A generation ago, when the New Math swept the country it had a pretty firm foundation at levels 1 and 2, but what little evidence we did gain at Level 3 showed us that teachers were actually subverting the New Math, preferring to bring in the Old Math whenever they could.

So, even if you are convinced that the theory behind some new program is sound, and even if you have seen reported evidence of controlled studies in classroom settings that are supportive of the theory's application, you're still not home free until you have seen the results of evaluation studies that indicate that this program really works in large numbers of regular classrooms.

Now you may be thinking that this represents quite a few gates for a new program to have to open before it proves its worth. And that is exactly the point! If we are to become less susceptible to fads, then it will be because we become more deliberate and cautious along the way to adopting new programs.

Figure 4.1 illustrates the process which ideally unfolds in the cycle of educational innovation. We begin with theories derived from pure or basic research. We test the theory under experimental or quasi-experimental conditions in school settings. We move from there to the program evaluation stage where assessment is made based on data from real classrooms which operate under typical day-to-day conditions.

We realize that these levels are in fact somewhat arbitrary, and we certainly do not maintain that there is necessarily a linear flow from pure to applied to evaluation research. Sometimes there is, but more often the situation is more chaotic than that. In some cases, the theoretical construct is less the source of energy than is the simple fact that something is available for educational use that was not available previously. Computers are an obvious example of this.

"IT PAYS TO BE IGNORANT" (OR DOES IT?)

Years ago there was a show on the radio called "It Pays to Be Ignorant." The theory behind the show was that people would win cash prizes and major household appliances by proving to the world, or at least to the huge nationwide radio audience, that they really were ignorant when it came to answering questions put to them by the genial host of the show. It was a great concept and a successful program, but we wish to say as clearly as possible that it doesn't pay to be ignorant when it comes to spending the public's tax dollars on educational innovations that really haven't proven themselves!

In the world of prescription medications, the Food and Drug Administration (FDA) subjects new medicines to a long and exhaustive review prior to allowing them to be prescribed by doctors and dispensed by pharmacists. Some critics of this system have pointed out that in many cases it takes years from the time we read about an experimental drug in the newspapers to that drug's release to the market. The role of the FDA is to play gatekeeper as tests are conducted, effects examined, potential drug interactions investigated, and so on.

As a result, some drugs never make it to the market place.

With respect to educational innovations, however, we have no counterpart to the FDA. Therefore, programs can be rushed into the schools with little or no testing at any stage of the game. This may please those who are in a hurry to jump on the latest bandwagon, but it disadvantages those who would prefer to be consumers of thoughtfully tested and refined programs. In so many instances, whole districts have adopted particular curriculums and teaching procedures that had basically no research foundation. This renders our profession vulnerable to criticisms that are difficult to refute.

In this chapter we suggest that research ought to be conducted at three distinctly different levels along the way to validating or invalidating educational innovations. Those three levels consist of (1) basic or pure research, (2) applied research in school settings, and (3) evaluation research where the effects of the large scale implementation of an innovation are studied. All of this takes time, and rightly so. We think that the only way to improve educational practice is to approach educational innovation with such a deliberate, measured sense of its worth.

Of course, schools adopt new ideas on the basis of something more than educational research. Economic, political, and cultural considerations will always play a role in this process. We have no problem with that. That is part of your reality and ours. But where we can be more thoughtful about change on the basis of a thorough examination of the merits of a given change, we ought to proceed cautiously.

USING EDUCATIONAL RESEARCH

As you consider restructuring your school, it is probably inevitable that you will hear claims or become the recipient of demands based on what educational research has to say. We encourage you to be cautious in this area because many are deceived about what is really there. The remaining chapters of this book will aid you by providing research-related findings for each of the restructuring topics, at least to the extent that research is available. In this regard, we provide a synopsis of the quantity and quality of the research at Levels 1, 2, and 3.

However useful this information may be, we feel impelled

to sound a cautionary note. No new idea, no matter how well researched, has meaning outside the context of purpose. For example, if we were asked, "Is an interdisciplinary curriculum a good idea for my school?," we would ask you, "What is the purpose of your attempt to restructure?" No one can answer that question meaningfully except the people who have a genuine interest in your school. Only those who really are affected by what happens there (teachers, administrators, students, parents) should even attempt to work through the process of deciding. If this seems wrong-headed in a day in which outside experts are readily available, just take a moment to consider the lessons of the history of failure and disappointment in educational innovation. Failure can more often than not be traced back to an initial confusion of purpose. It becomes compounded when the people who have the most to gain or lose are left out of the process. The outcome is cynicism and the "we tried that" syndrome.

Somewhere in the matrix of your individual and school goal structure you must take the measure of any new educational idea. The more meaningful question is not "is it good?" but "is it good for us?" Each educator and each person who cares about the school's welfare must ask the same basic questions:

- What does our school stand for?
- What should students learn?
- What are the best conditions for learning?
- What teacher behaviors enhance learning?
- How should classes and schools be organized?

. . . and so on. The questions are endless because:

- Teaching is as much an art as a science.
- Students are diverse and respond differently.
- Societal needs and demands change.
- Local and site-specific needs differ considerably.

The model we have illustrated here is just that—a model. Models are simplifications of reality and have their limitations.

THE FOLLOWING CHAPTERS

In the remainder of this book we examine a number of innovations currently put forth in the name of educational restructuring. For each of the topics we provide an overview, definitions, and examples. We recognize that in a country this large regional differences exist with regard to terminology, and some schools and districts occasionally define terms on a local basis. Such minor anomalies aside, we capture the essence of each of trend in the sense of its intent as portrayed in the published literature. Following our descriptions of practice, we examine the potentials and pitfalls of each given trend using the restructuring model described in Chapter 2. Following that we examine the research base for each of the practices using the 3-levels model described earlier in this chapter, and, where appropriate, we conclude our look at each topic by suggesting a research agenda to be carried out in a continued search for validation.

We have not included topics arbitrarily. For us to have considered a topic it must be a "major player" in the journals and in staff development activity, and on the agendas of major education conventions. No doubt we have left out certain topics dear to the hearts of some. *C'est la vie.*

REFERENCES

Bruner, J. (1966). *Toward a Theory of Instruction.* Cambridge, MA: Harvard University Press.

Ellis, A.K., & Fouts, J.T. (1993). *Research on Educational Innovations.* Princeton Junction, NJ: Eye on Education.

Gardner, H. (1986). *Frames of Mind.* New York: Basic Books.

Piaget, J. (1960). *The Child's Conceptions of the World.* Atlantic Highlands, NJ: Humanities Press, Inc.

5

OUTCOME-BASED EDUCATION[1]

By designing our educational system to achieve clearly
defined exit outcomes, we will free ourselves from the
traditional rigidity of schools and increase the likelihood that
all students will learn.

William Spady

We have spoken as if aims could be completely formed prior
to the attempt to realize them. . . . The aim as it first emerges
is a mere tentative sketch. The act of striving to realize it
tests its worth. . . . But usually—at least in complicated
situations—acting upon it brings to light conditions which
had been overlooked. . . . An aim must, then, be *flexible*. An
end established externally to the process of action is always
rigid.

John Dewey

I would argue that models such as mastery learning or
outcome-based education can function at the levels of
training and instruction, but they contradict the idea of
education as induction into knowledge.

James McKernan

---

[1] Portions of this chapter appear in our earlier book *Research on
Educational Innovations* (1993), and are used with permission of the publisher,
Eye on Education, Princeton Junction, NJ.

What is Outcome-Based Education?

Outcome-Based Education (OBE) is a "culminating demonstration of learning" (Spady, in Brandt, 1993). That is to say that OBE focuses on identifying and defining specified educational results and teaching toward them. Those results could include micro-outcomes, such as specific skills and information, and/or macro-outcomes, such as complex performance or interpretive abilities. OBE advocates distinguish between "enabling outcomes" which are the building blocks or benchmarks along the way and more often associated with mastery learning, and "exit outcomes" which are identified as larger, more complex capabilities and understandings that emerge from the cumulative effects of the smaller learning pieces.

William Spady, of OBE fame, maintains that our current educational paradigm is backwards. He cites custody and the calendar as the decisionmaking forces that drive our system. He writes that "school decisionmaking, curriculum planning, instructional and administrative operations" are all determined by the calendar. School year, semesters, units, credits, class periods, and so forth are the driving forces. Blocks of time have become the way of assessing student success or failure in the system. One could go on: students must stay in school until they are 16 years old, state laws require a minimum number of days in the school year, a certain number of hours per week in reading and math, etc. This is the stuff of bureaucracy, not the right stuff.

Spady (in Brandt, 1993, p. 66) notes that OBE can be briefly described on the basis of four defining principles:

> The first, in shorthand form, is *clarity of focus*. That means that all curriculum design, all instructional delivery, all assessment design is geared to what we want the kids to demonstrate successfully at the "real" end—not just the end of the week, the end of the semester, the end of the year—but the end of their time with us. Principle number two is *expanded opportunity*. It means expanding the ways and number of times kids get a chance to learn and demonstrate, at a very high level, whatever they are ultimately expected to learn. Number three is *high expectations*, which means getting rid of the bell curve. We don't want bell curve standards, expectations, and results; we want all kids able to do significant things well at the end. The fourth principle is *design down*: design curriculum back from where you want your students to end up.

A PRESCRIPTION FOR SCHOOL MALADIES

OBE is proposed by its advocates as a cure for our schools' bureaucratic ills. Spady defines OBE in the following way: "Outcome Based Education (OBE) means organizing for results: basing what we do instructionally on the outcomes we want to achieve; whether in specific parts of the curriculum or in the schooling process as a whole (Spady, 1988, p. 5)." The terms, "organizing for results" and "success for all," have emerged as trademarks of the OBE movement, which now has more than 2,000 member schools in its Network for Outcome-Based Schools founded in 1980.

Another definition, this one from the Far West Laboratory for Educational Research and Development, states that OBE is "a comprehensive approach to teaching and learning and to instructional management that has its roots in the Mastery

Learning and Competency-Based Education movements of the early 1970s" (Murphy, 1984).

Several philosophical premises underlie OBE practice, but four themes are always present. The first theme is that almost all students are capable of achieving excellence in learning the essentials of formal schooling. Teachers and administrators must truly believe this premise in order to make OBE a reality. Even though this first theme seems reasonable enough, in fact most teachers and administrators probably do not believe it. They will, therefore, have to redirect their thinking away from the traditional idea that some are capable of excellence, many of mediocrity, and some of failure.

The second OBE theme is that success influences self-concept; self-concept influences learning and behavior. The implication of this theme is not only that academics and affect are related but that there is a cause and effect relationship with academic achievement being the cause and improved self-concept being the effect. And in time, they begin to support each other so that the relationship is reciprocal.

The third theme is that the instructional process can be changed to improve learning. The perceived problem with the instructional process as it presently exists is that objectives and measured outcomes are often unrelated. Therefore, instruction continues apace and tests are given aplenty, but they are essentially unrelated processes which yield unreliable results. Students receive little or no corrective feedback and reinforcement along the way so that they often have scant idea of how they are doing in any kind of formative sense.

The fourth theme is that schools can maximize the learning conditions for all students by doing the following:

◆ Establishing a school climate which continually affirms the worth and diversity of all students;
◆ Specifying expected learning outcomes;
◆ Expecting that all students perform at high levels of learning;
◆ Ensuring that all students experience opportunities for personal success;
◆ Varying the time for learning according to the needs of

each student and the complexity of the task;

◆ Having staff and students both take responsibility for successful learning outcomes;

◆ Determining instructional assignments directly through continuous [formative] assessment of student learning;

◆ Certifying educational progress whenever demonstrated mastery is assessed and validated.

REVERSING THE ORDER OF THINGS

The traditional school-practice paradigm is one of writing objectives for a curriculum which is already in place or which has undergone some degree of modification. OBE turns the paradigm on its head. See Figure 5.1 in this regard. Note the near reverse order of things.

FIGURE 5.1. TWO EDUCATIONAL SYSTEM PARADIGMS

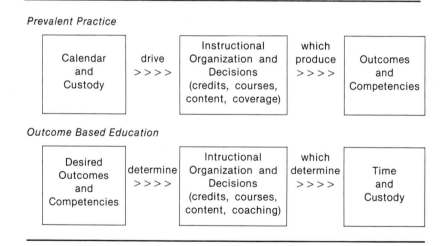

Prevalent Practice

| Calendar and Custody | drive > > > > | Instructional Organization and Decisions (credits, courses, content, coverage) | which produce > > > > | Outcomes and Competencies |

Outcome Based Education

| Desired Outcomes and Competencies | determine > > > > | Intructional Organization and Decisions (credits, courses, content, coaching) | which determine > > > > | Time and Custody |

In OBE the curriculum and the resulting educational experiences flow from the **outcomes** that you and your colleagues have determined are crucial. This is called the design-down principle by OBE people. That is to say, one begins by thinking about the loftiest outcomes possible long before one specifies the tasks and tests of school life. How that is different from beginning with goal statements, as some people have done for years, we aren't sure. Advocates of outcome-based education would answer that although people claim to have begun with goal statements for years, the fact that they seldom questioned the given axioms of school life (time, subject matter, custody, etc.) speaks for itself.

Figure 5.2 illustrates the design-down principle in which one begins with a clarity of focus on desired outcomes which then become the controlling factor in curriculum and instruction decisionmaking. If the outcomes are taken seriously, the thinking goes, then expanded opportunities and support for learning to truly happen must be put into place. This, as you might imagine, opens the door for mastery learning, generally a component of OBE.

FIGURE 5.2. OUTCOME-BASED DESIGN SEQUENCE AND GUIDING PRINCIPLES

Exit Outcomes > > > **Program Outcomes** > > > **Course Outcomes** > > > **Unit Outcomes** > > > **Lesson Outcomes**

- **Clarity of focus on outcomes.** Curriculum, instruction and evaluation should all be closely aligned with the desired educational outcomes. Students should always know what learning is expected of them and where they are in relation to the expected outcomes at all times.

- **Design Down from ultimate outcomes.** Curriculum and instructional decisions should be determined by the desired educational outcomes, rather than the other way around.

- **Expanded Opportunity and instructional support.** Content coverage is replaced by instructional coaching to ensure that the content is mastered, using formative evaluation, "second chance" instruction, and continual teacher encouragement and support.

- **High expectations for learning success.** The teachers' underlying philosophy is that all students can learn and expect high quality work from students. Consequently, students may are expected to redo substandard work, take incomplete, and retake tests when necessary.

Source: Spady, W.G. (1988), "Organizing for Results: The Basis of Authentic Restructuring and Reform," *Educational Leadership*, 46(2), p. 7.

Built into the equation as an element of belief or philosophy of OBE is the success principle. The success principle implies that all students can learn and produce work of good quality, although it may take some students longer or more repeated efforts to do so than others.

UNDERLYING PRINCIPLES

There are three major premises upon which OBE is founded. Those premises are: (1) all students can learn and succeed, not necessarily in the same way or at the same rate; (2) success breeds success (just recall the old saying that nothing succeeds like success); and (3) schools control the conditions of success. A measure of OBE's own success is the set of statements found in the National Goals for America's Schools which demand student outcomes at the center of improvement efforts.

The idea that all students can learn the curriculum traces back to the work of John Carroll who wrote a most intriguing article for *Teachers College Record* in 1963, titled "A Model of School Learning" (Carroll, 1963). Carroll's thesis, which in time was adopted by Benjamin Bloom, was that the issue is not *whether* a student can learn the curriculum, but the length of time it might take the student to learn it. Carroll suggested that we have confused time with ability, unwittingly rewarding those who are able to keep up with the daily flow of events and punishing the slower (not necessarily less intelligent) students. Thus all, or nearly all, students can learn the 3rd grade mathematics curriculum, for example, but they will naturally learn it at different rates. This ought not to surprise us, but apparently it does given the way schools are controlled by time. And that becomes one of the central arguments of OBE: by reconceptualizing our sense of purpose we are able to determine what we really want to accomplish.

The second premise of OBE, that success breeds success, is something that each of us knows experientially. Some research has shown (Walberg, 1984) that the motivation to learn academic subject matter is primarily the result of prior learning. In other words, the rich get richer and the poor get poorer. OBE enthusiasts point to success for every learner as something that needs to be built into the goal structure. Who could argue?

The third premise of OBE, that schools control the conditions of success, is depressing if one thinks of the realities of school life for many children who walk down the lonely road of failure every day. On the other hand, it is an empowering idea if one thinks of the possibilities. Again, the idea is that by reconceptualizing our very sense of purpose, we will think in terms of success for all rather than in terms of a competitive system where learning is treated as a scarce resource available only to a few. Still, it is probably both narrow and naive to think that schools control the conditions for success. They may be a major player, no doubt they are for many, but to say they control the conditions is to potentially give them more praise and/or blame than they ultimately deserve.

TRADITIONAL, TRANSITIONAL, TRANSFORMATIONAL OBE

Like all movements, OBE is differentially implemented in real world situations. At present there appear to be three versions of what OBE means to school personnel. The purest form, and the one touted by Spady, is Transformational OBE. As the word transformation implies, this form of OBE calls for a complete restructuring of the schools. Existing curriculum models, instructional systems, and methods of assessment would necessarily be replaced as dictated by the desired outcomes identified by school personnel. Anything less than this represents compromise with the old ways of doing things, and, of course, in such circumstances one always risks the possibility of making great efforts merely to perfect a mistake.

Let us digress into what we hope will be a meaningful example. If a desired outcome of the school experience is that students will think spatially, geometry comes quickly to mind. The reason this is so is because geometry is already in the curriculum, and it always has been. But maybe, just maybe, a course in architecture and design would get students to the desired outcome more readily than geometry. So, in a true transformation, all bets are off. The existing curriculum must carry the burden of proof against the desired outcomes. It's a rather refreshing idea in many ways. Among the notable school districts presently committed to Transformational OBE are Jefferson County, Colorado; Ferndale, Michigan; Syracuse, New York; Birmingham, Michigan; Aurora, Colorado; and Aberdeen, South Dakota.

At the other extreme is the form of OBE called Traditional. It is widely used today. The starting point for school districts using the Traditional form is the existing curriculum. Spady notes that this should more properly be called CBE, or Curriculum-Based Education, because the curriculum as it exists dictates the planning process. Here one would ask, "How can geometry help our students think spatially?" In one sense, this form serves the role of "straw man" which gets beaten up by the OBE purists as playing more of a confusing than a clarifying role in educational reform.

In between the two extreme forms one finds Transitional OBE. Whether this form is analogous to the ill-fated attempt to "transition" Americans to the metric system of a few years ago (remember the highway signs that listed both mph and kph?), or whether it is a useful way to wean school systems away from the academic-discipline domination of traditional curriculum to clarifying outcomes in advance, is problematic.

IMPLEMENTING OBE

The OBE implementation process begins with a commitment on the part of administrators, teachers, parents, and community to clarifying educational outcomes for students. Here planners are encouraged to think as grandly as possible about the goal structure of education. This stage is crucial because it is here that planners have the opportunity to reinvent the purpose of the school. All subsequent decisions about materials, learning environments, grades, etc., flow from the goal structure for better or for worse.

Once the goal structure is secured, one enters the second stage of OBE, that of aligning the curriculum with a set of objectives. As basic and obvious as this seems, it isn't. This is so because the objectives are at least theoretically freed from the constraints of tradition. So now, having begun anew, we are able to close the gap between what we say will happen and, indeed, what does happen in classrooms.

Within actual classrooms OBE is tolerant of a variety of teaching/learning strategies, but almost always mastery learning for each student is emphasized. Keep in mind that mastery learning is in fact method neutral. Of course, it is far easier to "prove" mastery on the basis of text, worksheets, etc., than it is to document it where students are doing projects and activities; but that is an age-old problem. Student achievement, however, becomes the determining factor rather than time, schedule, etc.

EVALUATING OBE

POTENTIAL AND PITFALLS

To be fair to OBE's potential, one must focus on its Transformational form. To do otherwise, merely makes the critics themselves vulnerable to the comeback that anything less (Traditional, Transitional) is really a half-hearted effort and probably doomed to failure. As any sincere would-be reformer will tell you, changing schools is extremely difficult and not as easy as saying, "We will now do OBE." Nevertheless, when school personnel decide that they will adopt an outcome-based approach to developing or changing their school, OBE seems to be among the more compelling ideas. This is particularly true if a school can free itself of bureaucratic, legal, and custodial constraints, and adopt the transformational model proposed by Spady.

OBE is basically bureaucratic, goal-oriented restructuring, with reasonable potential to arrive at fundamental restructuring. Transformational OBE elevates the process to the level of fundamental, goal-oriented restructuring shown in Quadrant I of the model presented in Chapter 3, Figure 3.4. Transitional OBE comes perilously close to moving the restructuring efforts out of Quadrant I and into another quadrant, depending on the results of the restructuring effort. Traditional OBE may result in bureaucratic changes, but seldom will it result in fundamental changes in what students learn and the way in which they learn it. By definition OBE is a goal-oriented process, but this element can become lost by a mandate given by administrators that OBE is to be used. Without the genuine agreement of all who will be affected on the underlying philosophy and driving forces behind OBE, the actual results of the efforts may end up in Quadrant IV, arbitrary bureaucratic changes to please an authoritative driving force for reform. With its three different models, OBE illustrates rather well the concept that an idea may fail for the wrong (bureaucratic) reasons as well as for such reasons as, "We tried it and it simply did not work." Traditional and Transformational OBE may well not represent sufficiently fundamental changes to overcome the complex inertial structure of schools as they presently are.

Recent criticisms of OBE (in any of its forms) have centered on its behavioristic, reductionist world view of education. As researcher Jim McKernan (1993, p. 343) of the University of Limerick in Ireland notes, "education is a social-reflexive process that must be negotiated in classrooms on a daily basis. No amount of 'teacher-proof' curricula, tables of specifications, scope and sequence charts, or lists of objectives can change these facts." McKernan's main point of contention seems to be that OBE lends itself rather well to *training* but not to the more subtle, complex nature of *education*. He writes further: "Imagining a student of *Macbeth* purchasing a text that includes all the possible interpretations and understandings of that play. . . . To cite the significant outcomes in advance of teaching and learning is absurd (p. 346)." McKernan's objections are not easy to walk away from, and his well-stated arguments are representative of the difference one finds between the experiential/process tradition of John Dewey, Jerome Bruner, and Eliot Eisner on the one hand, and the behaviorist/reductionist tradition of Frederick Winslow Taylor, Ralph Tyler, and Robert Mager on the other.

William Spady (1988) writes that "Outcome-based practitioners start by determining the knowledge, competencies, and qualities they want students to be able to demonstrate when they finish school. . . ." The statement has an eerie quality to it upon some reflection. First of all it is deterministic, reductionist, demanding of overt behaviors ("demonstrate"), and other-directed ("*they* want") rendering students as objects and not subjects as the process of education. We merely ask you to read the statement carefully and to reach your own conclusions.

THE RESEARCH BASE FOR OBE

Actually there is next to nothing to report at the basic or pure research level. Curiously, OBE makes no direct claims here that we could find. We would say, however, and this represents some interpolation and inference building on our part, that the theory of reductionism is at work here. By that we mean that OBE defines success as increased achievement as reflected by higher standardized test scores. Given the OBE operational definition of success which we noted earlier, and given that objectives are re-reduced toward alignment with test content, we can reasonably assume a reductionist world view.

At Level 2, or the classroom/school level, mastery learning serves as the linchpin of OBE. There is a considerable body of research to be found here, and it is rather good research. Walberg (1984), Bloom (1984), and others present findings in the forms of individual studies, research reviews, research syntheses, and meta-analyses (Guskey & Pigott, 1988; Kulik & Kulik, 1986–87; Guskey & Gates, 1986; Stallings & Stipek, 1986; Walberg, 1985). The consensus is one of efficacious outcomes when it comes to raising test scores. There is a general acceptance among key researchers that mastery works. The only point of dissent is one raised by researcher Robert Slavin (1987), who perceptively points out that test score gains were derived from short-term studies. He notes that studies of over 4 weeks' duration show no educationally significant differences over other approaches. This is a very important consideration because teachers must think long-term if we are to make real improvements in academic outcomes.

At Level 3, or the level of actual program evaluation research, we find many stories about schools and whole districts that have been "turned around" by OBE. Given the previously addressed definition of success as improved test scores, we encounter claims from the far-flung outposts of empire: Johnson City, New York; New Canaan Connecticut; Red Bank, New Jersey; Sparta, Illinois; and the list goes on. The fact that test scores have improved is a hard fact to walk away from given the manifold woes of American schools. What is not clear is the quality of these program evaluations. They are largely unpublished and otherwise unavailable for critical review. They could range from those of excellent design and execution to mere "gee whiz" stories.

We remain convinced that much of what is embedded in Outcome Based Education is largely unproven. The biggest problem seems to be the tendency to "oversell" OBE. Why not just look at the several simple and reasonable premises upon which OBE is actually founded? And why not expect (and take part in it for that matter) that Level 2 research be carried out so that we can gain some useful insights to classroom applications of OBE? The fact remains that there is little that is new here, and the echoes of such predecessors as competency-based education are more than clear.

A RESEARCH AGENDA FOR OBE

In one sense, OBE does not lend itself to research because it is not a particular program. It is, rather, a planning/designing approach for identifying appropriate educational outcomes. The appropriate strategies or instructional/curricular programs needed to attain those outcomes are a matter of discretion. Therefore, the empirical results of an outcome approach would represent the variable effects of the implementation of different programs at different schools. For example, one school might identify a number of academic outcomes suitable for university admission, while another school might identify a set of more vocational-related outcomes. But to say this and merely to let things go at that is to be somewhat disingenuous about the matter. The fact is that OBE claims, admittedly in some cases indirectly, that it will bring about improved achievement. Otherwise, why do it? One searches the OBE literature for alternative claims such as more happy classrooms, more cohesive learning environments, or improved landscapes of penetrating thought, all to no avail. Let's face it, if OBE cannot deliver higher test scores, it has little claim on our time, money, interest, and affection.

What OBE does allow researchers to do is to begin with a clear set of learning outcomes to be evaluated. The research can then be directed toward evaluating the outcomes designed in the planning process. This clearly makes Level 2 and Level 3 research much easier. OBE can and should be researched at the school level (Level 2) using qualitative, ethnographic research methodologies to determine the degree to which the process is followed and the results are actually realized. The resulting "knowledge, competencies, and qualities . . . students [are] able to demonstrate when they finish . . ." (Spady, 1988) can readily be researched using quantitative and qualitative methods. An evaluation plan, whatever form it takes, must be developed in such a way that evaluation is aligned with objectives and curriculum. When OBE is coupled with mastery learning in its more severe forms, the criticism is that teaching is to the test. But given the alternative, teaching and testing as unrelated entities, it might not appear to be so primitive. The point is, that when teaching is aligned with testing, the latter supposedly becomes a natural outgrowth of the former. Perhaps more than anything else, the OBE movement has focused our attention toward the meaning of validity in assessment, and this, itself, is a major contribution.

Level 3, or program evaluation research, is apparently a more elusive task. This is ironic because the subjects and their performances are available for study; in fact, the amount of money spent on new programs ought to demand that we collect good data from our curricular/instructional implementations. The problem is that those whose interest is in research data are often in a different world (the universities), and it's a shame the two groups don't collaborate more than they do. The question to answer at this level is eminently practical, "Do schools that follow an OBE model provide a qualitatively different (better) education than non-OBE schools?" What we are asking is whether the OBE model can be successfully employed on a large scale and transported to other schools with some confidence that it will work elsewhere? The anecdotalists would have us believe so, but we need to hear from the empiricists as well.

References

Bloom, B.S. (1984). The search for methods of group instruction as effective as one-to-one tutoring. *Educational Leadership*, 41(8), 4–17.

Brandt, R. (1992–93). On outcome-based education: A

conversation with Bill Spady. *Educational Leadership, 50* (Dec. 92/Jan. 93), 66–70.

Carroll, J.B. (1963). A model for school learning. *Teachers College Record, 64,* 723–33.

Guskey, T.R., & Gates, S.L. (1986). Synthesis of research on the effects of mastery learning in elementary and secondary classrooms. *Educational Leadership,* 43(8), 73–81.

Guskey, T.R., & Pigott, T.D. (1988). Research on group-based mastery learning programs: A meta-analysis. *Journal of Educational Research,* 81(4), 197–216.

Kulik, C.C., & Kulik, J.(1986–87). Mastery testing and student learning: A meta-analysis. *Journal of Educational Technology Systems,* 15(3), 325–41.

McKernan, J. (1993). Some limitations of Outcome-Based Education. *Journal of Curriculum Studies,* 8(4), 343–53.

Murphy, C. (ed.) (1984). *Outcome-Based Instructional Systems: Primer and Practice. Education Brief.* San Francisco, CA: Far West Laboratory for Educational Research and Development (ERIC Document Reproduction Service No. ED249265).

Slavin, R.E. (1987). Mastery learning reconsidered. *Review of Educational Research,* 57(2), 175–213.

Spady, W.G. (1988). Organizing for results: The basis of authentic restructuring and reform. *Educational Leadership,* 46(2), 4–8.

Stallings, J., & Stipek, D. (1986). "Research on early childhood and elementary school teaching programs." In *Handbook of Research on Teaching,* 3rd ed., edited by M.C. Witrock. New York: Macmillan.

Walberg, H.J. (1984). Improving the productivity of America's schools. *Educational Leadership,* 41(8), 19–27.

Walberg, H.J. (1985) "Examining the theory, practice, and outcomes of mastery learning." In *Improving Student Achievement Through Mastery Learning Programs,* edited by D.U. Levine. San Francisco, CA: Jossey-Bass.

6

SITE-BASED
MANAGEMENT

Restructuring and site-based management have become the
clarion call of educational reformers.

Paul Goldman, Diane Dunlap, David Conley

History tells us that tinkering with formal roles and
relationships will not make a significant difference in the
lives of teachers or students.

Terrence E. Deal

The transition from traditional patterns of faculty problem
solving and decisionmaking to more collaborative ones is
fraught with difficulties. . . . Teachers and principals
commonly compare their restructuring efforts to rebuilding a
747 while it's in the air.

Gordon A. Donaldson, Jr.

WHAT IS SITE-BASED MANAGEMENT?

There was a time when the typical American school was the heart of the enterprise, not part of a larger structure called a school district. It was locally owned and operated. The money to run the school came mainly from the community, and decisions were made locally. The school was an integral part of the community, woven into the fabric of daily life. The school was the site of the community theater, the big game, the senior prom, the polling place, and just about anything else of any significance in the shared life of the community. This is not an easy thing for people to understand today in an age of crosstown busing, politicized school boards, and national goals for education. But long ago and far away from today's realities that's the way it was.

Site-based management[1] is, more than anything, an argument for turning the decisionmaking processes over to local control. In 1989, the Chicago Public Schools embarked on a world-class example of site-based management. In effect, every Chicago public school became autonomous to the extent of electing its own Local School Council (LSC) comprised of parents, local residents, and school faculty. These councils are empowered with the authority to hire and fire principals, to consider and adopt curricula, and to modify schedules and other routines of school life (Fig. 6.1). Of course, a certain degree of centralization related to budgets, policies, etc., still exists. Nevertheless, this "experiment" represents a serious attempt to restructure much of the day-to-day processes of schooling.

The historically curious fact of the bold Chicago maneuver is that it came about just a century into a seemingly unstoppable wave of centralization and standardization of American public schools. According to historian Herbert Kliebard (1982), just before the end of the 19th Century a series of events took place changing the fundamental power structure

---

[1] The term *school-based management* is also a common term in the literature. We use site-based management and school-based management interchangeably in this chapter.

FIGURE 6.1. GUIDELINES FOR THE CHICAGO SCHOOLS' LOCAL
SCHOOL COUNCILS

Formation

◆ Each School must establish a Local School Council (LSC)
consisting of parents, community members, teachers,
and students.

Responsibilities

◆ Each school must have a School Improvement Plan (SIP)
approved by the LSC. The LSC is charged with
monitoring its implementation and reporting publicly
twice a year.

◆ The LSC consults with the principal on the school
budget and may direct the allocation of money within
budget funds.

◆ The LSC selects and evaluates the school principal.

◆ The LSC advises the principal on a variety of matters
involving school functioning, such as the allocation of
certified and uncertified staff at the school, staff
appointments, attendance and disciplinary policies, and
curriculum and textbook selection.

◆ The LSC must insure the school complies with state and
federal regulations pertaining to schools and LSC
governance.

Source: Chicago Public Schools, Office of Reform (1993). *LSC Sourcebook: Basics
for the Local School Council.* Chicago, IL: Board of Education of the City of
Chicago.

of the schools. The effect of the change was to shift the
educational center of gravity away from faculty and the texts
they selected as the source of the curriculum to a knowledge-
and decisionmaking base that was more remote. The
exponential increase in the sheer numbers of students and the
increased complexities of society's demands on the schools
seemed to call for both standardization and centralization of
policies. School districts encompassing large numbers of

individual schools came into being. Superintendents were hired; so were deputy superintendents. Each state built its own educational bureaucracy and so did each district within each state.

Numbers of different schools specialized by grade and age levels were needed in each community. To accommodate these expansions, school boards adopted set curricula, policies, etc., and decisionmaking became further and further removed from the individual schools. Faculty no longer decided curricular and other matters. The teacher's function narrowed to that of deliverer of curriculum. Teachers came to view their own classrooms as their territory where before they had held a wider, school-encompassing view of their responsibilities.

In time, funding for schools grew gradually to depend more on the state rather than on the local community. Today the breakdown is roughly 50% state, 45% local, and 5% federal financial support. As this happened, state mandates came to predominate. Funding and control generally go hand-in-glove. State bureaucracies developed to dictate how money was to be spent, setting policies, guidelines, and curriculum requirements that all schools were expected to meet.

By the 1960s the power base had been so effectively removed from those most closely associated with a particular school (the teachers, administrators, and parents) that everyone no doubt thought it had always been this way. This situation led to an inflexibility that has made substantive change at any given school difficult to say the least. So far removed is the locus of control today, that most of us merely take for granted the many federal mandates (P.L. 94–142, busing, Title This and Title That) that come our way.

Now on center stage among the many current reform efforts in education is an attempt to reverse this decades-old trend called site-based management. As much as anything, restructuring has come to mean returning decisionmaking authority to the local schools. As the term implies, "site-based management" means that each school will manage it own affairs, leaving only certain legal matters to central authority. The movement has generated no shortage of terms: *decentralization, school or site-based management, and participatory or shared decisionmaking*. Regardless of the term, the intent is the same: To free schools to respond more quickly and more realistically to the needs of the students under the direction of those most closely associated with a particular school.

Researcher Kathleen Cotton (1992) has concluded that despite the variety of terms and approaches there is general agreement on certain aspects of school-based management. Cotton notes that the common threads include a shift of authority from central offices to local sites with the individual school faculty and constituency as the primary decisionmaking agents (Fig. 6.2).

FIGURE 6.2. COMMON THEMES IN VARYING DEFINITIONS OF SITE-BASED MANAGEMENT

Is a form of district organization.

Alters the governance of education.

Represents a shift of authority toward decentralization.

Identifies the school as the primary unit of educational change.

Moves increased decisionmaking power to the local school site.

Source: Cotton, K. (1992). *School-Based Management (Topical Synthesis #6).* Portland, OR: Northwest Regional Educational Laboratory.

The professional literature of the past several years is filled with articles on site-based management: rationale, strategies, case studies, anecdotal stories, and practical steps to its fulfillment. A search of the ERIC database for the subject heading "school-based management" for the years 1982 to 1993 resulted in no less than 890 entries. We have attempted to sift through this ever-increasing stack of paper in a search for the salient points. In so doing, we have come up with the following thoughts which we detail by paragraph.

KEY ELEMENTS

The key elements of site-based management seem to include a range of activities formerly dictated by central offices and school boards. Various degrees of site-based budget control permit alternative uses of funds, a vital psychological and real factor in restructuring. Teams consisting of faculty and community members usually form the decisionmaking corps, with key roles allotted to parents, students (especially at the high school level), principals, and teachers. The school curriculum itself is often the focus of elaborate decisionmaking, and in many cases each school selects its own course of study, at least within state-required regulations. Schools are generally encouraged to establish a sense of identity, to show how they are unique, and to express a particular philosophy and goal structure of education, often in the form of a school charter. In some cases, this results in requests for waivers from regulations that might inhibit local creativity. And schools that elect site-based management are almost always required to account for progress and improvement in the form of an annual report (Cawelti, 1989).

KEY QUESTIONS

The move by any school which has been part of a larger district structure to site-based management is a difficult transition. We advise any faculty/community group that might be considering such a move to ask themselves the following questions: Why do we desire site-based management? How do we define site-based management? Who will be included? What powers are negotiable with the district and state? How will roles be defined? What rights and responsibilities emerge from such a change? Will training be necessary? If so, for whom and in what forms? What are the unique characteristics of our situation? What conditions must be present and guaranteed in order for site-based management to work in our situation? What can we learn from others in the public and private sectors (inside and outside education) about making this transition (Harrison, Killion, & Mitchell, 1989)? Of course, there are other questions, but these will do for starters.

ADVICE FOR IMPLEMENTATION

J.T. Lange's (1993) advice to those considering site-based management makes sense to us. Lange points to 10 ideas for faculty and community members to think about as they move in this direction. These ideas appear in Figure 6.3. If nothing else, the reader will appreciate something between the lines, and that is the time factor. There simply is no way around this issue. Because site-based management is inherently more democratic and localized, it will make great demands on the time and energy of those involved. We think this is without a doubt the most problematic issue at stake in the entire process. Every teacher and administrator we know tells us that he/she is already working at capacity and beyond. Where the time will come from for the endless meetings, consultations, votes, and exchanges of opinions, we are not sure.

EVALUATING SITE BASED MANAGEMENT

POTENTIAL AND PITFALLS

Site-based management (SBM) is often touted as the linchpin of the restructuring movement. It has become so closely aligned with restructuring that the two have almost become inseparable. SBM in its purest form is clearly bureaucratic restructuring, although it may have the potential for true fundamental reform of education. It is pleasing to think that the teachers and administrators who work most closely with students will be empowered to make decisions about curriculum and instruction. Freeing schools of bureaucratic red tape is an appealing idea, and no doubt some teachers would be able to do a much better job if given more freedom. To truly make a difference however, SBM must show that closing the gap between the decisionmaking process and the day-to-day realities of school life will result in academic improvement and increased "customer" satisfaction.

While SBM may have the potential to lead to the fundamental reform of education in and of itself, it is simply bureaucratic reform that probably will not result in a fundamental reformation. There are several assumptions on which the current SBM movement is founded, and each one of them is fraught with eminent peril. Let's examine those assumptions.

FIGURE 6.3. ADVICE ON IMPLEMENTING AND POTENTIAL PROBLEMS WITH SBM

---

1. Advice on Implementing

◆ The primary motive for initiating site-based, shared decisionmaking should be the desire to improve scholastic achievement and student success.

◆ Total district acceptance and commitment should be promoted if shared decisionmaking is to be successful.

◆ Strong alliances should be forged with employee groups.

◆ Time should be taken in the planning phase.

◆ Once the definition, policy, and regulations are agreed upon, formal adoption should occur.

◆ Upon board approval, in-service training should begin immediately.

◆ Because shared decisionmaking is inefficient, decisionmaking arenas should be established.

◆ Those involved should be kept current on the latest research regarding both school administration/ management and teaching and learning.

◆ Provisions should be made for site-based options and for waivers from restrictive rules and bargained agreements.

◆ As roles change and time requirements become more demanding, matching salaries to new responsibilities must be evaluated.

Source: Lange, J.T. (1993). Site-Based, Shared Decision Making: A Resource for Restructuring. *NASSP Bulletin* (January), 101–05.

2. Potential Problems With SBM

◆ Lack of time and a feeling of being overloaded on the part of teachers.

◆ Lack of clarity regarding roles, definitions, and purposes.

◆ The need for more training in the areas of budgeting, team building, and instructional improvement.

◆ The reverting to old ways of doing business by teachers and administrators.

◆ Lack of adequate funding.

Source: Wood, F.H. & Caldwell, S.D. (1991). Planning and Training to Implement Site-Based Management. *Journal of Staff Development, 12* (3), 28–29.

First, SBM is based on an assumption that teachers are interested in fundamental restructuring of education. While some teachers may be, our admittedly biased sample tells us that there are schools where the majority of teachers really are not. They are traditionalists in the strongest sense of the word. Empowering those teachers or schools will not lead to fundamental changes in what and how students learn. It may, in fact, merely confuse their role, leaving them somewhere in a no-man's land between teacher and administrator. More than one teacher, confronted with the responsibilities inherent in site-based management, has said, "Just leave me alone and let me teach."

Second, there are those critics of education who believe that teachers' beliefs about education are part of the problem, not part of the solution. If the teachers had the solutions, so this line of thought goes, the schools would not have the problems they do. Turning the schools over to those who have helped create the problems will not solve the difficulties. As the writer R.E. Young (1990) once noted, "Those . . . who seek to breathe new life into the role of schooling have failed to realize that the methodology they seek to use is responsible for the problems they want to solve."

Third, there is an assumption that a faculty of teachers and administrators and their local constituency can readily agree on a *meaningful and coherent* educational philosophy. There are schools where this has happened, but there are also schools where this has failed because of the very differing philosophies of the participants. The fact is that schools, as they are presently staffed, seldom can point to an agreed upon set of principles and goals. In Holland, we have observed, schools of choice are based on a coherent world view shared by faculty, parents, and students. Without such agreement, why even consider site-based management? Without such agreement, fundamental changes will be few, and "reform" that takes place will be superficial indeed.

Fourth, there is an assumption that districts and states will actually abdicate meaningful control to local schools. Without this, site-based management becomes a farce and a superficial effort at reform. A key difference between the local control of the last century and attempts to return to it in modern times is a difference as basic as where the money comes from. Long ago, the money was local money. Today it is state money. It is difficult to separate sources of money from sources of power, certainly more difficult than a little good will can bring about.

THE RESEARCH BASE FOR SITE-BASED MANAGEMENT

The Level 1 research or theoretical base for site-based management is found in organizational theories derived from the business world. Textbooks on educational administration borrow freely from these business models, all of which are offered as ways to get the organization to operate most successfully, which ultimately means profitably. While there is a growing number of education textbooks devoted to organization, most contain theories and practices that have their origins in the world of business and industry. So it is by metaphor and analogy that we entertain ideas of site-based management for school settings.

Robert Owens' text, *Organizational Behavior in Education* (1991), describes the polar ends of a continuum on which are found two competing theoretical models. Owens uses the terms bureaucratic theory and human resources development theory for these two fundamentally opposing models. The bureaucratic theory is the traditional hierarchical model complete with top-down management and decisionmaking. It is based on a perception of the average worker as someone who lacks the expertise, desire, or ability to be involved in important decisions. At the other end, human resources development theory holds the opposite view of human nature; it teaches that personal, and therefore institutional and organizational effectiveness is increased when those on the "lower rungs" are involved in the decisionmaking process. Much of this thinking rests on the works of such theorists as Douglas McGregor (Theory X and Theory Y), Rensis Likert (4 Systems of Management), and Chris Argyris (Pattern A and Pattern B leaders). Each of these theories advocates inclusion, reflection, decisionmaking, and local control. Obviously, site-based management falls into this latter theoretical camp.

Research on site-based management focuses on three specific questions. Since site-based management is neither a curricular nor an instructional treatment *per se*, it is not something that fits neatly into the category of experimental, or Level 2 research. In lieu of experimental studies, educational researchers have focused on perceptions of site-based management. Specifically, the following descriptive or ethnographic research questions have been addressed:

◆ The nature of site-based management, what is it, how is it being implemented, what are the problems?

◆ How do participants feel about site-based management?

In the absence of controlled experimental studies, what has been examined to a limited degree, are the changes, if any, in student achievement in those schools where site-based management has been implemented, a type of Level 3 research. These studies address the research question:

◆ How does site-based management affect student learning?

The answer so far is mainly that we do not know. The jury is still out, and the verdict is yet to be rendered.

The nature of site-based management dominates the

literature and examples of this type of writing are found in Figure 6.4. How much of this is actually high quality descriptive research and how much is anecdotal is difficult to determine, although our guess is it leans toward the anecdotal end of the spectrum. What is clear from the abundance of materials available on SBM is that there are wide variations in how the concept is actually being implemented in the schools. Decentralization and local decisionmaking are the common denominators. But that isn't much to go on.

The ultimate question for site-based management proponents is the third question listed earlier. If student performance is not enhanced, then site-based management may be just another bureaucratic effort at restructuring that has failed to affect student learning in a meaningful way. The research in this area is not extensive; neither is it of high quality. In fact, we have found few *published* research articles even addressing this question. The evidence is slim to none at Level 3 that student learning has increased at schools that have adopted site-based management. Others who have looked at the evidence using numerous unpublished program evaluations have reached similar conclusions:

> Thus far, researchers have identified no direct link—positive or negative—between school-based management and student achievement or other student outcomes, such as attendance. In some settings, student scores (on standardized or local tests) have improved slightly, in others they have declined slightly, and in most settings no differences have been noted (Cotton, p. 9).

> In sum, research as a whole does not indicate that site-based management brings consistent or stable improvements in student performance (Peterson, 1991, p. 2).

FIGURE 6.4. RESEARCH FINDINGS ON PARTICIPANT ATTITUDES ABOUT SITE-BASED MANAGEMENT

◆ **School staff members** generally perceive their schools as being more responsive under decentralized arrangements, with responsiveness defined as the ability to adapt resources and procedures to student needs. However, enthusiasm for SBM on the part of school staff has been shown to decline if the practice continues over a significant period of time and few or no improvements are noted in working conditions or student outcomes.

◆ **Parent and student** satisfaction with the schools has been shown to increase under school-based management.

◆ **Principals** have consistently shown a high degree of satisfaction with the move to school-based management, even though they also say that their workload has increased.

◆ **Teachers** want to be able to make or influence decisions regarding curriculum and instruction and have often reacted negatively to participation in decisionmaking about organizational matters that bear little relationship to the classroom.

◆ **Site Council** members express resentment (1) if allowed to make decisions only about trivial matters, or (2) if their decisions have only very minor impact on school policy and operations, or (3) if they are told they are a decisionmaking body, but then have their decisions vetoed by the principal.

Source: Cotton, K. (1992). *School-Based Management (Topical Synthesis # 6)*. Portland, OR: Northwest Regional Educational Laboratory, pp. 8–9.

A RESEARCH AGENDA FOR SITE-BASED MANAGEMENT

The majority of the research on site-based management thus far has focused on process and not product. Our review of the literature on this topic shows that there is an abundance of materials on what to do, how to do it, and what to avoid. At some point the research must link SBM to student outcomes in a more direct manner. After all, improved student outcomes represent a major reason for the whole restructuring movement. And yet, so far, SBM has not been shown to be effective to this end. Our agenda for SBM is the same as it is for any other bureaucratic reform effort.

Level 3, or program evaluation research, is crucial to the coming of age of our profession. The question to answer at this level is very similar to the one we articulated for OBE, "Do the students at a school that implements a site-based management/decision-making model receive a qualitatively different (better) education than do students who attend schools following the traditional model?" Much of the research has focused on the process of implementation. It is time to answer the more difficult, more important question: Does site-based management lead to improved student learning?

REFERENCES

Cawelti, G. (1989). Key elements of site-based management. *Educational Leadership, 46*(8), 46.

Cotton, K. (1992). *School-Based Management (Topical Synthesis #6)*. Portland, OR: Northwest Regional Educational Laboratory.

Harrison, C.R., Killion, J.P., & Mitchell, J.E. (1989). Site-based management: The realities of implementation. *Educational Leadership, 46*(8), 55–58.

Kliebard, H.M. (1986). *The Struggle for the American Curriculum: 1893–1958*. Boston: Routledge and Kegan Paul.

Lange, J.T. (1993). Site-based, shared decisionmaking: A resource for restructuring. *NASSP Bulletin* (January), 98–107.

McGregor, D.M. (1960). *The Human Side of Enterprise*. New York: McGraw-Hill Book Company.

Owens, R.G. (1991). *Organizational Behavior in Education (4th ed.)*. Englewood Cliffs, NJ: Prentice Hall.

Peterson, D. (1991). *School-Based Management and Student Performance* (ERIC Digest No. 62). University of Oregon: Clearinghouse on Educational Management.

Young, R.E. (1990). *A Critical Theory of Education: Habermas and Our Children's Future*. New York: Teacher's College Press.

7

TOTAL QUALITY MANAGEMENT

I want you to know that for me Deming is the last great
leader of the Enlightenment. . . . He's provided the final, and
missing, element of natural law.

Anonymous middle school civics teacher in Sioux City, Iowa

It is disturbing that educators have rushed to TQM as the
potion for education's ills. . . . Educators should beware of
being seduced by the siren song of TQM.

Colleen Capper and Michael T. Jamison

. . . Behind the high-stepping OBE jargon of transformational
outcomes, learning paradigms, and empowerment lurk
behaviorist methods that are totally at odds with the Deming
quest for quality.

Maurice Holt

What is Total Quality Management?

Total Quality Management (TQM) is a theory of process improvement conceived in the 1930s by the American industrial psychologist W. Edwards Deming. The goal of TQM is to enhance the quality of the process leading to a given product, and in so doing, to enhance customer satisfaction. TQM theorist Deming's principles were adopted by the Japanese after World War II, helping to change the world's perception of "Made in Japan" from one of derision to one of admiration. Ironically, Deming's ideas were long ignored by U.S. businesses. Recently, however, they have gained widespread acceptance throughout this country.

More than once in our educational history, innovators have looked to the business/industrial world for cues to how to improve the schools. It is, therefore, not surprising that TQM, with all its highly-touted success stories from business and industry, should show up on the doorsteps of our schools seeking entrance. Enthusiasts have come up with a slight twist, Total Quality Education (TQE), but the essence remains the same. Once again we find ourselves indebted to the business community for providing us with a philosophical premise for school improvement. In fact, business metaphors and business influence in general are deeply imbedded in 20th Century American education. For example, Maurice Holt (1993) observed:

> If one had to name the single biggest influence on American Education during this century, a strong candidate would be not John Dewey but Frederick Winslow Taylor, the father of "scientific management. . . . School Boards quickly picked up ideas from Taylor's 1895 book, *Shop Management*, which recommended using product specifications to define standards of output performance (p. 382).

Taylor's model was, of course, one of social efficiency or social engineering. But its influence can hardly be overstated. So pervasive are social efficiency protocols in school life that they are merely taken for granted rather than thoughtfully examined. They include such accepted procedures as lesson plans, behavioral objectives, classroom management procedures, and the whole range of standardization theorems such as graded classes, clock hours, time-on-task, etc. Recently, educational innovators turned away from efficiency models while remaining reluctant to turn away from business itself as a way out of our troubles. Deming's TQM ideas offer a distinctly different alternative because they are (1) inclusive rather than top-down in their approach to decisionmaking, and (2) localized rather than centralized in terms of the locus of the power base. In this respect they reflect much of the same philosophy on which site-based management is founded, and which we mentioned in the last chapter. For example, many of Deming's ideas are perfectly compatible with McGregor's Theory Y of decentralized, inclusive leadership management over traditional centralized, top-down boss-management.

At the heart of Deming's theory are some very fundamental beliefs about human nature and organizations. Deming holds a positive view of human nature, that is, he is convinced that human beings have an inherent desire to achieve and perform successfully. But he is equally convinced that traditional management structures and approaches work against and limit these desires. In this sense, Deming sees that the problem is with the organization and how it is configured and not with the individual. The remedy, as he sees it, is for organizations to focus on the process. Quality must be a process long before it becomes a product. If the process is about quality, a quality product will follow. The task of leadership is to communicate a common theoretical orientation of inclusion and empowerment to all of the members of the organization, and to use it as the driving force in organizational decisions and functions.

In some ways Deming's process-linked emphasis is reminiscent of Jerome Bruner's (1960) educational theory which attempted to place the accent on the processes of education rather than merely on the products. Bruner suggested in no uncertain terms that what happens along the way in learning is probably more significant than the product itself. He called for a new generation of curricular and instructional approaches which emphasized active student learning through such methods as discovery, inquiry, and sensory and intuitive learning. Bruner was the most articulate spokesman for the 1960s versions of New Math, New Science, New Social Studies, etc. Today, however, few educators remember or are even aware of Bruner's work, leaving us once more in the deficient position of attempting to recreate our own history from a foundation of ignorance. Of course, Deming's emphasis is different from Bruner's in that Deming focuses on management while Bruner focused on curriculum and instruction.

Deming, like Woodrow Wilson before him, proposed 14 points for quality. Those 14 points have become a beacon for educators as they attempt to implement his philosophy in school settings. The exact meaning of these 14 points seems rather variable as educators interpret them, but there appear to be some common elements of application. We have selected one interpretation that we think is fairly representative (Rankin, 1992) to present here. In essence, what Rankin is telling the reader is that serious positive change will result if a given school or district implements *all* 14 quality dimensions. At the heart of the list is the idea of total inclusion of the "work force," which would include, one supposes, not merely the professional work force, but students and their parents as well. Deming's 14 points (principles), which Rankin proposes be implemented, are shown in Figure 7.1.

The best known education-world link to TQM is William Glasser, M.D., who wrote *The Quality School* (1990). Glasser first came to notice in education three decades ago when he struck a responsive chord with his ideas about helping individuals gain greater control over their own lives. His book, *Reality Therapy* (1965), presented a convincing argument that each of us chooses what we do with our lives and that we are responsible for our choices. This obviously has great implications for teaching and learning, especially the elements of those pursuits related to discipline and responsibility. To the extent that Glasser's ideas have become fused with Deming's (and they have in the TQM/TQE movement), the model becomes reflective empowering, and therapeutic in nature. Glasser offers the theoretical underpinning so desperately needed to make the case for both teacher and student empowerment. His works are must reading for serious students of TQM.

FIGURE 7.1. DEMING'S 14 PRINCIPLES AND THEIR IMPLICATIONS FOR EDUCATION

---

1. *Create Constancy of Purpose.* Customers must be clearly defined. System boundaries must be clear. The system must improve so that the customers receive quality education, benefit from continual improvement, and act in support of the system.

2. *Adopt the New Philosophy.* Existing methods, materials, and environments may be replaced by new teaching and learning strategies where success for every student is more probable.

3. *Cease Dependence on Inspection to Achieve Quality.* Educators should monitor the teaching process as it occurs and use feedback to adjust teaching methods and materials as needed. Educational measurement is more likely to be used to improve the teaching and learning process when it occurs as part of the ongoing instruction rather than at some annual testing period.

4. *Consider Total Costs. Do Not Trust the Low Bid on Each Item.* In education this principle may be appropriate to the purchase of textbooks and tests, computers, and other equipment and supplies. The important thing is to consider the total costs and benefits of the alternatives, not just their initial cost.

5. *Improve Constantly and Forever Every Process for Planning Production and Service.* The focus of improvement efforts, under a Deming approach, would be on the teaching and learning processes using the best research to suggest strategies then trying them out, studying and acting on the results. Standardized tests would become less used and substantial improvements would be needed in the measurement of those learnings that are measurable and in managing for the attainment of important learnings that are not measurable.

6. *Institute Training on the Job.* The school day should provide time for training that is directly related to improving instructional quality. There may be some greater costs to allow such training, but in the long run educational quality gains should more than make up for the costs.

7. *Adopt and Institute Leadership.* Education leaders must learn the same skills as leaders in industry, and they must learn to

carry out the same responsibilities. They need to eliminate such processes as standards, rating systems, quotas, and MBO, and learn to improve the system itself.

8. *Drive Out Fear.* Educational leaders must remove worry and fears, and work with employees on improving the processes. If the quality is not there, the fault, most likely, is in the system, not in the teachers and other workers. The focus of our improvement efforts must be placed on the processes and on the results, not on trying to make people accountable.

9. *Break Down Barriers Between Staff Areas.* This principle applies to interdepartmental cooperation. It also applies to interdisciplinary instructional efforts such as teacher teams, writing-to-learn programs that involve several subject areas, and student investigations of problems from different disciplines. It suggests the sharing of resources such as computers among the staff.

10. *Eliminate Slogans, Exhortations, and Targets for the Work Force.* Teachers and principals are intelligent, dedicated workers who can have internal motivation and can craft carefully-designed processes to improve teaching and learning. Lasting increases in effort derive from sterner stuff than slogans.

11. *Eliminate Numerical Quotas for the Work Force and Numerical Goals for Management.* Educational leaders must substitute leadership for quotas and focus attention on the processes rather than on the outcomes. Leadership must be substituted for numerical targets for principals and school in terms of attendance rates, failure rates, test scores, dropout rates, etc.

12. *Remove Barriers that Rob People of Pride of Workmanship.* Intrinsic motivation that is supported by the system is the best bet to engender pride of quality of workmanship. Merit systems are held in suspect by educators, tend to divide rather than unite, and are often no more deserved by one teacher than another.

13. *Institute a Vigorous Program of Education and Self-Improvement for Everyone.* Inquiring, vital educators who are up-to-date in their field and on current world issues are more likely to find quality solutions to instructional problems, and will surely make learning more interesting for students. The educational

system should view the continuing education of its staff members as an investment in educational quality for students.

14. *Put Everybody in the Company to Work to Accomplish the Transformation.* All the key parties in a school district must have substantial understanding of the system, and many of them will need specific training in advance of any decision to go forward. They must know the consequences of an agreement to transform their district using these principles, and be eager to do so.

Source: Adapted from Rankin, S.C. (1992). Total Quality Management: Implications for Educational Assessment. *NASSP Bulletin* (September), 66–76.

Further insight to school-related applications of TQM is furnished by Crawford, Bodine, and Hoglund (1993) who describe its liberating, empowering effects on its users, especially in contrast to traditional forms of management. They write:

> Whether the worker is the employee in the factory, the student in the classroom, or the teacher in the school, the psychological effects of boss management are the same: It deprives the individual of innate motivation, self-esteem, and dignity while cultivating fear and defensiveness. The result is loss of motivation to quality work (p. 53).

In their book, *The School for Quality Learning*, they articulate the paradigm shift that they suggest will take place as schools move from traditional boss-management styles to the lead-management style of TQM.

TQM VS. OBE

Holt (1993) builds a very strong case that TQM is qualitatively different and philosophically opposed to another highly-touted innovation, Outcome-Based Education (OBE). OBE, he claims, is product-driven while TQM is process-driven. This is a fundamental distinction that educators too often fail to make, as we pointed out earlier with reference to Jerome

Bruner's thoughts on curricular and instructional emphases. Holt writes, "In short, the curriculum determines the assessment, exactly as it should from Deming's standpoint and exactly as it does not with outcome-based education." (Holt, p. 387). OBE, Holt insists, is based on "visible numbers," the profit line, while TQM rests on the professional judgment and assessment of teachers.

Curiously, it is not at all uncommon to find both TQM and OBE being touted by the same individuals, even though they are, in our opinion, contradictory in nature. Some districts are bound and determined to incorporate all of the hot topics into their school restructuring efforts, contradictions be damned.

Holt's perceptive comments indicate to us that many restructuring efforts are not driven by a clearly articulated educational philosophy, but rather by the desire to do things because they represent the "latest trend." The philosopher Francis Bacon noted this human fallacy some centuries ago, calling it the "Idol of the Tribe." Latterday commentators have called it "getting on the bandwagon," or "everyone's doing it."

The strange marriage of OBE and TQM has its supporters, and one group has even given it a name: "Outcomes-Based Decision Making" (Melvin, 1991). There does not appear to be a clearly articulated underlying philosophy to this action, but that has not stopped the rush to innovation in the past, and it probably won't stop it in the future. Perhaps such a maneuver can be defended on an eclectic basis, but there is little indication that those who combine the two are even aware of the opposing energizing philosophies on which each is founded. Such atheoretical approaches certainly run contrary to Deming's position of the importance of the constancy of philosophy within an organization.

CRITICISMS AND WITTICISMS

Reviews of TQM in the literature are few, possibly because it has not been around long enough, well-enough understood, or applied in enough key settings to attract the attention of critics. It seems to be a rapidly spreading phenomenon with few serious critics at this point. There is, however, some activity.

Capper and Jamison (1993) base their criticism of TQM on a social reconstuctionist view of education. They write, "when the yardstick of social reform is rigorously applied to TQM, . . . it appears simply to be a new and interesting arrangement of deck chairs on the *SS Titanic* (p. 27)." Yes, perhaps, but social reform represents a very big yardstick, taking into account the measure of the whole of society and not merely that portion that lies within the province of the schools. If learning and not social reform is the goal of education, this objection might well be open to question.

Another critic, Sztain (1992), objects to the business metaphor, presenting a logical argument that metaphors can become self-fulfilling prophecies. She argues that an economic model, even that of an enlightened corporation, is inappropriate for the schools. She may very well be right, and we find her attention to language compelling. Metaphors *do* effect how we think and act once we accept them as labels. The 18th Century educator Fredrich Froebel gave our profession a stunning metaphor, one that has continued to be a philosophical lodestar, when he put forth the idea of a kindergarten, or children's garden, as a place of learning for the young. But the objections to TQM are few and far between at this point.

EVALUATING TOTAL QUALITY MANAGEMENT

POTENTIAL AND PITFALLS

TQM and its educational application (TQE) represent a restructuring approach that focuses on totally revamping the school bureaucracy, based on a specific philosophy of human nature. The underlying premise is the belief that the trouble with schools in America stems from the bureaucratic structure and the deleterious effects it produces. Suppose that TQM/TQE could be implemented in a pure form in a random sample of 100 schools in the United States using existing personnel, and in a variety of communities. Would the classrooms of these schools be fundamentally different from those using traditional approaches? It is pleasing to think so. It is appealing to think of teachers as internally motivated, empowered decisionmakers. It is compelling to imagine that this empowerment would result in real fundamental changes in education. The potential appears to be there. And by the way, if we were truly serious in our attempts to restructure, such a pilot study of randomly selected sites using reasonably controlled conditions would be the way to test the idea.

At the same time, some potential pitfalls are worth noting. Many of the concerns are the same concerns we have regarding site-based management. TQM is based on an assumption that teachers and administrators are genuinely interested in the fundamental restructuring of education. While some teachers may be, we have worked with schools where the majority of teachers really are not. They are traditionalists in the strongest sense of the word. Empowering those teachers or schools will not lead to fundamental changes in what and how students learn. It will result only in tinkering with the way things are. In fact, there are those who are convinced that teachers' beliefs about education are part of the problem, not part of the solution. In order for TQM to work, a complete change in philosophy is necessary. The danger is that the philosophical foundation will never be completely understood by some. Changing philosophies is hard, and enthusiasm for change is no substitute for substance.

A very problematic issue, and one that is seldom addressed in our experience is the assumption that a faculty of teachers will readily agree on any *meaningful and coherent* educational philosophy. Think for a moment about the faculty of any given school. Rarely is there anything approaching unanimity in terms of a world view. In the more concrete world of business and industry, it is, by comparison, easy to get workers to agree that we need to improve our product against that of the competition. There are schools where philosophical opinion is relatively agreed upon, but there are far more schools where it is not. Consequently, fundamental changes are few, and reform is superficial.

A third issue is that of real control over one's destiny. There is an assumption that districts and states will actually turn over meaningful control to local school sites. With states controlling on average about 50% of school revenues, it remains to be seen how far they will go in allowing a given school to chart its own course.

It must be recognized that elements of TQM philosophy are at direct odds with most other drives for reform. Performance-Based Education (PBE), OBE, America 2000 goals, and calls for national assessment are trends that are not necessarily compatible with the underlying philosophy of TQM. As a result, schools who try to meld these other elements with TQM face the very real danger of constructing an incoherent philosophy as the basis for reform.

On the other hand, even industry itself cannot completely call its own shots in spite of the movement to TQM. To take the automobile industry as an example, car makers must comply with federal and state regulations regarding fuel consumption, exhaust emissions, safety standards, and a host of other constraints. Any efforts a given automobile corporation makes toward TQM must be taken within those guidelines. So if TQM/TQE is it succeed in the schools, it, too, will find its measures of autonomy within state or federal guidelines.

Finally, we return to what is to us the most troubling issue. Educators must once again address the question of the appropriateness of relying on a business model to drive education. In our opinion the losses have outweighed the gains of such alliances in the past. Our early models of school and its purposes came from the Greek word *schole*, the closest English translation of which is "leisure." The idea was of a place devoted not to efficiency, but to a gathering of students and teachers who wished to think about and exchange ideas.

THE RESEARCH BASE FOR TQM

The Level 1 research or theoretical base for TQM is based on the work of Deming. It is a brilliant, elaborate, and very defensible construct, similar in many ways to the theoretical basis of site-based management. It comes from organizational theories derived from business and industrial psychology as we have noted.

Robert Owens' *Organizational Behavior in Education* (1991), for example, describes two ends of a spectrum representing two competing theoretical models. Owens uses the terms bureaucratic theory and human resources development theory. The bureaucratic theory is the traditional hierarchical model with top-down management and decisionmaking, based on a view of that the average worker lacks the expertise, desire, or ability to be involved in important decisions. At the other end, the more person-centered theory holds the opposite view of human nature, suggesting that personal, and, therefore, institutional and organizational effectiveness is increased when those on the "lower rungs" are involved in the decisionmaking process. It all rests on such theoretical constructs as Douglas McGregor's (1960) Theory X and Theory Y, Rensis Likert's (1961) 4 Systems of Management, and Christ Argyris' (1957) Pattern A and Pattern B leaders. We think these are insightful theories that have been proven to be useful in the world of business and industry.

The research base for TQM is quite similar to the research base for site-based management. Like site-based management it is not given to typical educational research procedures. It simply is not something that fits neatly into the category of experimental, or Level 2 research. At this point, most of the research being done on TQM is descriptive in nature and focuses on how the concepts are being applied in various school settings. There are the usual variety of articles that contain anecdotal reports of its efficacy in increasing learning (for example, Schmoker and Wilson, 1993; Bonstingl, 1992), but it is probably too early to expect quality research on educational outcomes.

In a manner reminiscent of the attitude of Whole Language enthusiasts, the TQM/TQE people have thrown down the gauntlet with their dismissal of standard research measures as means to determining the effectiveness of what they propose. Consider, for example, this quote from Crawford, Bodine, and Hoglund (1993, pp. 227–28): "We have stressed the irrelevance of standardized tests for assessing learning outcomes in the school for quality learning. Second, the narrow criteria of standardized test scores confirm only the learning that occurs in school and only fragmented, measurable pieces of that in-school learning."

If, as Crawford and friends say, standardized tests are irrelevant measures of learning, then we have a major problem on our hands. Perhaps they have a point. Standardized tests have come under fire from a variety of quarters in recent times.

But the questions of (1) what we should replace them with, and (2) how claims of comparative effectiveness can reasonably be made in their absence are enormous questions.

What cannot be ignored is the bottom line in the business world, and there "research" or at least the apparent outcomes of TQM seem indisputably efficacious. Japanese industry, in particular, has led the way, and a number of American companies (for example, Xerox, Chrysler, and General Motors) report great success as a direct result of TQM. The degree to which this "research" can be generalized to education is the $64 question. Students are not factory workers, and test results are not durable goods. Nevertheless, when something is so compelling in one form of human endeavor, it is at least worth considering in another. If TQM/TQE has come to the world of education as metaphor and analogy from business, then what precisely are the analogs of increased worker involvement and improved customer satisfaction?

A Research Agenda for Total Quality Management

The ultimate question for TQM proponents and the profession is whether student learning and satisfaction is enhanced. If it is not the case, then TQM is just another bureaucratic effort at restructuring that has failed to reach the levels of fundamental issues. The research in this area is not extensive because it is a relatively new (for education) idea. In fact, we have found few quality *published* research articles which thoughtfully address this question. But we ought not to be surprised because TQM is a very difficult thing to research. Isolating the TQM variable is not easy, and may not even be possible for a number of reasons including:

◆ It is not a solitary entity, that is, it is a philosophical policy position, and, therefore, will manifest itself in a variety of ways when implemented.

◆ As it is being implemented in most places, it is being used with a variety of other restructuring concepts. For research purposes, this presents what is called a confounding effect.

◆ In spite of TQM's best efforts, state and district policies may prohibit its implementation in a meaningful way.

◆ TQM downplays the focus on traditional outcome measures, making actual changes difficult to assess, at least through the use of standardized tests. This makes it a tough nut to crack.

We will continue to maintain that it is the job of Level 3 (program evaluation) researchers to address these problems in their designs, and it must be done by those who are serious about school restructuring. Undoubtedly the research will continue to focus on process and not product, but that may not be enough for educational policy makers. Our review of the literature on this topic shows that there is a growing abundance of print telling educators what to do, how to do it, and what to avoid. The research on process is important, but may not be enough. TQM philosophy doesn't say not to examine the end product, but that it should not drive the process. Good evaluation research can do both.

REFERENCES

Argyris, C. (1957). *Personality and Organization: The Conflict Between the System and the Individual.* New York: Harper & Row.

Bonstingl, J.J. (1992). The quality revolution in education. *Educational Leadership, 50*(3), 4–9.

Bruner, J.S. (1966). *The Process of Education.* New York: Vintage Books.

Capper, C.A., & Jamison, M.T. (1993). Let the buyer beware: Total quality management and educational research and practice. *Educational Researcher, 22*(8), 15–30.

Crawford, D.K., Bodine, R.J., & Hoglund, R.C. (1993). *The School for Quality Learning.* Champaign, Illinois: Research Press.

Deming, W.E. (1993). *The New Economics for Industry, Government, Education.* Cambridge, MA: MIT Center for Advanced Engineering Study.

Glasser, W. (1990). *The Quality School.* New York: Harper & Row.

Glasser, W. (1965). *Reality Therapy.* New York: Harper & Row.

Holt, M. (1993). The educational consequences of W. Edwards Deming. *Phi Delta Kappan* (January), 382–88.

Leading indicators—Assorted facts and opinions for recent research on American education (1992, Spring). Agenda: America's Schools for the 21st Century.

Likert, R. *New Patterns of Management.* New York: McGraw-Hill.

McGregor, D.M. (1960). *The Human Side of Enterprise.* New York: McGraw-Hill.

Melvin, C.A. (1991). Restructuring schools by applying Deming's management theories. *Journal of Staff Development,* 12(3), 16–20.

Owens, R.G. (1991). *Organizational Behavior in Education* (4th ed.). Englewood Cliffs, NJ: Prentice Hall.

Rankin, S.C. (1992). Total quality management: Implications for educational assessment. *NASSP Bulletin* (September), 66–76.

Schmoker, M., & Wilson, R. (1993). Transforming schools through total quality education. *Phi Delta Kappan* (January), 389–95.

Sztajin, P. (1992). A matter of metaphors: Education as a handmade process. *Educational Leadership,* 50(3), 35–37.

8

YEAR-ROUND SCHOOLS

In the 1800s and early 1900s, the agrarian calendar for student attendance was important when over 85% of the people were engaged in agriculture. . . . Today, conditions have changed with less than 3% of the work force engaged in agriculture, the agrarian calendar is outdated and has outlived its time.

James Bradford, Jr.

We are unable to generate tax dollars to build schools at the rate needed. Does it make any sense that millions of dollars in school buildings stand idle for three months a year?

Norman Brekke

. . . Practical experience has shown that most of the instructional methods used in year-round education are the same as in traditional education.

Gary L. Peltier

WHAT ARE YEAR-ROUND SCHOOLS?

The concept of year-round schools has been around seemingly forever. In one form or another it dates back at least to the turn of the century. Year-round schools cropped up in Bluffton, Indiana, in 1904, Newark, New Jersey, in 1912, Minot, North Dakota, in 1917, Omaha, Nebraska, in 1925, Nashville, Tennessee, in 1926, and Alquippa, Pennsylvania, in 1928. They came and they went. Always, they have been presented as a way to break ranks with the agriculturally-based school year. People have pointed out that few children are involved in the berry harvest anymore, so why not put them in school where they can learn something.

The restructuring of education in the 1990s has brought about renewed attention to this idea which is, apparently, too tough to die. And it does seem to be enjoying a renaissance of sorts. The National Association for Year-Round Education reported that in the 1991–1992 school year, 23 states had some form of year-round schooling, involving 1,668 schools and over 1.3 million students (Bradford, 1991). One year later the number had grown to 26 states, and 2,049 schools, a 23% increase over the previous year, and a 135% increase over 1990 (Ballinger, 1993). There seems to be a trend here.

The call for year-round education is not the result of a single force. It comes from readily recognizable but rather distinctly different corners of the educational establishment. Like so many other educational innovations, it is supported by a coalition of boosters. One group has economic concerns and is convinced that year-round schools will save the taxpayers money, and another is convinced of year-round schools' instructional/learning advantages. A third group argues that most kids simply do not have anything purposeful to do in the summer, and it is, therefore, the schools' responsibility to take care of them. These concerns are different, but they are not necessarily antithetical one to another.

THE CONCERN WITH ECONOMY

An undeniable fact of American education is that most schools sit idle for 2 to 3 months of the year. There may be some summer school activities at a few sites, but these are usually optional programs involving only a comparative handful of students. For one-quarter to one-third of the year these multimillion dollar facilities are vacant. One could argue that *if* the buildings were used more efficiently, a school district with 20 school buildings would need only 15. Or a district with 15 schools currently at capacity enrollments and projected growth to 20 schools would not need the additional schools if the buildings were used 12 months of the year. Depending on how they are configured, year-round models allow from 33% to 50% more students to use the system *without* building additional schools.

The economic incentives and possibilities have not been lost on school boards and superintendents struggling to make ends meet in the face of growing student populations. Although these financial savings have been questioned (Rasberry, 1992), a range of calendars have been developed by districts in efforts to avoid building new schools. The most common plans are described in Figure 8.1. Many of these plans do not call for *more* days of school for any given student. Rather, they call for staggered attendance schedules which allow a school to accommodate greater numbers of students over the course of a year. Some, noting the longer attendance year in Japan (220 days), Russia (210 days), and other nations, call for a school year with more attendance days than the typical American child (180 days) currently experiences.

Although economic concerns are paramount, proponents of year-round schools also point to certain educational benefits. While the evidence of educational benefits is inconclusive and problematic, it is a *fact* that many school districts have gone to year-round scheduling to avoid new building construction.

THE CONCERN WITH LEARNING

Alongside the economic concerns are the perceived educational benefits derived from year-round education. There

---

FIGURE 8.1. COMMON CALENDAR OPTIONS FOR YEAR-ROUND EDUCATION

Quarter Plan divides the calendar into 4 12-week periods of time: Fall, Winter, Spring, Summer. Students may select, or are assigned to any combination of three of the four quarters.

45–15 Block Plan or single block plan, divides the year into 4 9-week terms, separated by 4 3-week vacations periods. The entire student body begins together, usually in July, and attends for 9 weeks and on vacation for 3 weeks. The pattern is repeated throughout the year.

45–15 Staggered Plan is the same as the 45–15 block plan, except that vacations are staggered throughout the year. Each "track" of students has its own vacation schedule. With four tracks of students, only three of the tracks are in school at any one time, meaning that 33% more students can attend the same building.

Concept 6 Plan provides for six terms of approximately 43 days each, with students attending four of the six terms, sometimes with longer school days to substitute for slightly fewer school days. This plan divides students into three groups, with one group always on vacation, meaning a 50% increase in the number of students who can attend one building.

Trimester Plan calls for three equal semesters throughout the year, with students attending two of the three trimesters. Independent study or more time in school each day may be required to meet state minimum attendance laws.

Quinmester Plan offers 5 9-week terms, with students attending four of the five. This model has been particularly popular at the high school level because summer school programs are easily converted to a 9-week term.

Other plans which include various components of the above include the **60–20 Block or Staggered, 90–30 Staggered, 60–15, Orchard, Concept 8, Concept 12, Concept 16,** and **Multiple Access** plans.

Source: Adapted from Mussatti, D.J. (1992). *Year-Round Education: Calendar Options*. ERIC Reproduction Service No. ED343278.

are two different but related ideas that generate this argument. One is the benefit derived from the elimination of the long summer break, what might be called the "forget factor," something teachers in traditional programs encounter every fall when students return to school. The other is the expansion, at least in some models, of the number of attendance days. This 3 month hiatus is seen as a relic of an agrarian society, a drawback to learning for many children, particularly those from lower socioeconomic classes and from other-language homes. Year-round school provides continuous learning throughout the year, elimination of summer losses due to extended vacations, and ample opportunities between sessions for remedial and accelerated work. These reasons are usually cited by proponents even when the driving force behind the year-round school calendar is economics.

Most models of the year-round school maintain the traditional American 180 days of instruction. There is, however, a concern and desire on the part of some to lengthen the school year. James Bradford (1991), a Virginia superintendent and president of the National Association for Year-Round Education writes:

> Despite the many needs of America's youth, the United States continues to have the shortest school year (180 days) of any other industrialized nation. In most of the European countries the school year is at least 220 days. Japanese children attend school for 240 days each year, and Russian children attend school for 210 days each year.
>
> The primary reason given for not changing the school calendar is that of tradition and a cliché that quality is more important that [sic] quantity. I remind you that learning does take time, and for some children learning will require more time than it does for others. . . . The long summer vacation is an outmoded system for educating America's children. . . . The traditional or agrarian calendar has outlived its time and now is the time to change the school calendar to a system of continuous learning and reflect the lifestyles of the parents in the 21st Century (pp. 5–6, 10).

The literature on year-round schools shows that proponents cite both the educational and economic advantages in their attempts to build a case. In fact, other reasons are also given, such as enhanced teacher salaries (Gandara, 1992), compatibility with American family lifestyle (Bradford, 1991), reduced vandalism, and increased attendance of students and teachers (Ballinger, 1993).

It should be pointed out that year-round education is not popular with many people, and the public is not at all sold on it. Yet, like wing-tip shoes it always seems to be around, never dominant but never completely out of style either. It enjoyed a temporary surge of enthusiasm in the late 1960s and early 1970s. Many schools and districts that have tried it have gone back to the old schedule (White, 1992) for a variety of reasons which are summarized in Figure 8.2, the most compelling of which seems to be inertia.

EVALUATING YEAR-ROUND EDUCATION

POTENTIAL AND PITFALLS

Changing the school calendar is a bureaucratic restructuring maneuver that has gained some popularity in recent years. At this point it hardly qualifies as a trend that is sweeping the country. The extent to which it might lead in time to fundamental changes in the system is open to question. Certainly an extended school year has its selling points because more time spent in teaching and learning seems a reasonable thing, especially with other-language students and the socially and economically disadvantaged. Monetary savings as a result of decreased demand for more school buildings is hardly a trifling matter. But other than that, the arguments do not appear to have sufficient momentum behind them to bring this issue to the forefront. Perhaps in time that will change.

There is a danger that an inordinate focus on the school calendar as a primary restructuring effort takes attention away from more pressing questions about teaching and learning. If a student is learning information and skills of questionable value in 180 days or 220 days, over 9 months or spread over 12 months, what difference does it make? One of the ironies from

---

FIGURE 8.2. MOST COMMONLY CITED REASONS FOR AND AGAINST YEAR-ROUND SCHOOL

Pro:

◆ The traditional calendar is antiquated and based on an agrarian society no longer dominant in the United States.

◆ American students need an extended calendar and additional school days to be able to compete internationally with the lengthened school years in other countries.

◆ Disadvantaged students need the additional schooling during the summer months.

◆ The problems with student retention over the long summer vacations will be alleviated with the opportunity for continuous instruction and learning.

◆ Year-round schedules will save money, particularly in school construction, and lessen the overcrowding in schools.

◆ The shorter between session vacations can be used for remediation and acceleration activities for many students.

◆ Teacher salaries are enhanced because of longer school years and more school days.
School vandalism is reduced with a year-round schedule.

Con:

◆ Family summer vacations and plans are disrupted.

◆ There is no evidence that students learn more on year-round schedules.

◆ Administrator and teachers are subject to burnout with year-round schedules.

◆ Financial savings are minimal.

◆ Scheduling of courses is extremely difficult, particularly at the secondary level.

◆ Opportunities for summer employment of older students are minimized.

◆ Tracking systems often result in children in the same family having different vacations.

◆ There is insufficient time for school maintenance and repairs.

---

the fabled *Nation at Risk* (1983) document was the contradictory conclusion that the school year should be extended, the authors having already pointed out what a poor job we were doing. If a student attends an impersonal, stagnant school environment for 9 or 12 months, the results probably will not differ much.

Taken alone, scheduling changes will probably make little difference. As a part of a restructuring effort, the move to year-round schools may make sense, but out of context and merely tossed into the vast complicated matrix of school life, it is a bureaucratic change, and as the history of its abandonment shows, a superficial change. We agree with Rasberry (1992) who points out that shifting days of attendance does not get at such fundamental elements of restructuring as increased parent involvement, a restructured curriculum, improved teacher development, and research-supported instructional techniques.

EDUCATIONAL RESEARCH AND YEAR-ROUND EDUCATION

Published research and program evaluation studies of good quality on this topic are rare. There are claims in the popular literature about the efficacy of such programs (*e.g.*, Bradford, 1992), but such enthusiasm, admirable as it is, should not be confused with good quality published research. Most of the published articles are in fact position papers that tout the value, both economic and educational, of year-round school. Our review of the evidence has led us to conclude that in spite of the claims of educational advantages, the case is not convincingly made for greater academic achievement as a result of year-round schooling. This conclusion is reached by others who have examined the evidence (National Education Association, 1987; Peltier, 1991; Rasberry, 1992).

A RESEARCH AGENDA FOR YEAR-ROUND EDUCATION

Year-round education represents a policy move that changes

the school calendar from its traditional reliance on the agrarian cycle to one more in keeping with the need to provide adequate care and nurture for students all the months of the year. In a sense, it is an admission that where once young people were *needed* to help with the harvest, now they are not necessary.

We include this introductory paragraph because of our belief that year-round education (YRE) is driven less by philosophical or empirical knowledge than by the needs to use school buildings more efficiently and to keep our young people purposefully occupied during the day. Neither of these needs is trivial, so in that sense YRE needs no defense. It is also true that with the advent of large numbers of non-English speaking immigrants to the United States in recent years, the absence of English practice by children for up to 3 months every summer is a problem.

The problem with attempts to subject YRE to research investigation is that so many variables are subsumed under what is almost always a districtwide policy change. The fact that districts often make the change to YRE *because* of changing demographics, makes longitudinal comparisons within a district fraught with rival hypotheses. Achievement may well go down in a district where large numbers of non-English speaking families are incorporated into the schools, so a shift to YRE in such a case might show lower achievement, but it may have little or nothing to do with YRE.

Our suggestion to those considering YRE is that if the move is made, for whatever reasons, that: (1) attempts are made to survey parent, student, and faculty levels of satisfaction over time; (2) comparisons are made with past achievement in the district even though there may be mitigating factors; (3) achievement comparisons are made with similar districts not using YRE; and (4) data are collected on what are called educational indicators, including such factors as attendance, disciplinary referrals, percentages of graduates, dropout rates, numbers of students who continue on to post-secondary education, and follow-up studies of graduates.

REFERENCES

Ballinger, C. (1993). *Annual Report to the Association on the Status of Year-Round Education.* San Diego, CA: National Association for Year-Round Education (ERIC Document Reproduction Service No. ED358551).

Bradford, J.C. (1991). *Year-Round Schools: A National Perspective.* Franklin, VA: Franklin City Public Schools (ERIC Document Reproduction Service No. ED343259).

Bradford, J.C. (1992). *A National Model: A Voluntary Four-Quarter Plan at the High School Level.* Buena Vista, VA: Buena Vista Public Schools (ERIC Document Reproduction Service No. ED343261).

Gandara, P. (1992). Extended year, extended contracts: Increasing teacher salary options. *Urban Education, 27*(3), 229–47.

National Commission on Excellence in Education (1983). *A Nation At Risk.* Washington, DC: U.S. Government Printing Office.

National Education Association (1987). *Year-Round Schools. "What Research Says About:"* Washington, DC: National Education Association (ERIC Document Reproduction Service No. ED310486).

Peltier, G.L. (1991). Year-round education: The controversy and research evidence. *NASSP Bulletin, 75* (September), 120–29.

Rasberry, Q. (1992). *Year-Round Schools May Not be the Answer.* (ERIC Document Reproduction Service No. ED353658).

White, W.D. (1992). Year-round no more. *American School Board Journal, 178*(7), 27–30.

9

PARENTAL INVOLVEMENT

Parent-family involvement in public schools has now reached
a new level of acceptance as one of the many factors
considered to improve the quality of schools.

William Rioux and Nancy Berla

These are our children. We pay the taxes, which in turn pay
all the salaries of the teachers. . . . We expect modifications,
improvements, and accountability. We will no longer sit in
the wings, in fear of repercussions, and watch the years of
our children's education fly by.

Parents in Cortlandt Manor, New York, to the school board

Inviting parent participation is like throwing a rump roast in
to a shark tank; you're sure to get activity.

Bart "Stump" Morgan

What is Parent Involvement

In a more perfect world we wouldn't need schools. We wouldn't have to send our children to a specific site called school each day in the name of learning. In a more perfect world we wouldn't need schools, but we would need education. And just where would the young receive their education if there were no schools? They would receive their education from the community because the community owes its children an education. A child's community is made up first of the child's family, but also of the child's relatives, friends, neighbors, and the many community groups, clubs, agencies, libraries, museums, businesses, as well as the culture in general. The more integrated the elements of the community are, and the better they function, the more it is natural for a child simply to learn from the community just by being part of it. This is the sense of *paideia*. Paideia is a Greek word which means (roughly translated because there is no English equivalent) learning from the culture. Few would seriously suggest today that it would suffice merely to allow our children to prepare to become contributing adults by taking part in the culture at large. This is so because the culture is both dangerous and impoverished. The paradox is that school works well only when the larger culture works well. Somehow we want our schools to be "better" than the culture, to make up for its deficits, and to provide what it seemingly cannot provide, but that is probably not possible.

The German philosopher Jurgen Habermas (Young, 1990) has written about the rising "youth crisis" in the societies of the Western world. He lays much of the problem right at the feet of parents. Habermas suggests that children are confused over the growing sense of privatism displayed by their parents. He notes that while adults increase their demands for better conduct and performance on the part of government officials, they themselves continue to withdraw from community involvement. To take one example, just think about the amount of time you and other adults you know spend watching television. Surveys tell us that the amount of time varies from 1 to several hours per day on average. Regardless of how uplifting and educational those programs might be, they do keep us from doing other things. In other words, while you are watching television, you cannot be out in the neighborhood interacting with other people.

Habermas documents the shift away from public life by ordinary people to a life spent largely in what could be called private activities. He claims that our children sense this contradiction as they are continually exhorted to become participating citizens in a democracy. The decline of scouts, clubs, church activities, etc., that brought children together with good adult role models furthers the difficulty. These organizations were practice for participatory citizenship. Habermas suggests that they provided the transcendent moments that happen in groups where camaraderie, sharing, group effort, projects, etc., provide the experiences so necessary for a meaningful passage from childhood and adolescence to adulthood. They have been replaced by shopping malls, video arcades, MTV, and other wastelands that offer nothing of the shared experienced needed for citizens of a democratic society.

We have included this chapter on parental involvement because it is our feeling that if parents were more involved in the educational process of their children than they have been over the past few decades, much of the talk of restructuring schools would be unnecessary. The abdication of this parental responsibility to the state is one of the main reasons that schools are in the shape that they are in. Do not misunderstand us. We are not saying that parents should necessarily "school" their own children. The growth of the home schooling movement, however, should not be seen as an isolated event having nothing to do with the decline of education for the young. But we do believe that parents have the responsibility to be involved in the *educational* process. They simply must provide the guidance in the values that all children need to be successful adults in our society. And this means, in part, to stress the importance of learning and success in school.

We have been involved in a variety of international education projects, and one advantage of such experience is the opportunity to hear different points of view on seemingly ordinary matters. One Chinese educator we worked with, Dr. "Jack" C.K. Chan, commented that in his opinion Americans are very good at schooling their children, but they aren't very good at educating them. This individual had drawn a clear distinction between the formal schooling process (that is, getting in and getting out) and actually internalizing the vital values, knowledge, and insights necessary for leading a satisfying life and making meaningful contributions to society. It is the latter, he felt, that made a person truly educated.

It may well be that many parents have relegated the education of their children to the schools. School is an important part of a child's education, but school alone is not enough. This is rather clearly demonstrated in America today. Education is more than just making it through high school, college, or graduate school. Perhaps the following two examples will help demonstrate this point.

For years teachers and others have complained about the deleterious effects of summer vacation on student learning and retention. In fact, today one of the forces driving the year-round schools movement is the belief that an extended schedule will mean a safeguarding of the knowledge and momentum lost over the summer. This is a widespread belief, but the research evidence in this area shows that at best this belief is open to question. Heyns (1978) studied 2,978 Atlanta, Georgia, 5th and 6th graders in an effort to determine what happened to learning over the summer vacation. She concluded that, indeed, the very disadvantaged students lost ground in the summer time, but she also found that children from higher income families learned almost as much during summer vacation as they did during the year. This was thought to be due to activities such as traveling with parents, summer camps, and other "educational" activities, but the one activity that seemed to be most important was independent reading on the part of students. These informal activities, probably sporadic throughout the summer, appeared to provide learning equal, though different, to that provided by 6 hours a day of formal structured "schooling." It is well to recall that some of the best schooling ever devised, that which took place in ancient Athens, was considered to be a leisure pursuit. Notice we didn't say it was a leisure suit.

A second example is one that is well-known, but from which we seem to be reluctant to learn. We do not question that there are problems with American schools. Obviously changes are needed. Perhaps it is in spite of the educational system in which they find themselves, but there *are* students who do quite well in the schools and who are world-class achievers. They come from all the sectors of society, but an inordinate number of them are of Asian background (Stevenson, 1992). Why this is so is no secret. These children come from families that value learning, where parents instill a desire to learn and succeed. The parents are supportive and involved, often sacrificing their own wants and desires to their children's needs, an increasingly rare trait in today's world.

The lack of parental support and involvement has been addressed by American educators with a call for more funding and more programs. Such demands represent an attempt to provide an alternative to parental involvement to compensate for the failure of parents to help educate their children. However, it is our belief that institutions can never fully replace the role of parents. The alternative is to bring parents *into* the process of educating their children, rather than attempting to replace them. The success of Asian students, the vast majority of whom do not come from the upper classes, demonstrates that it is a question of the value of learning, and not economic status, that is important. This is what the current parental involvement programs are about.

Schools are better and students learn more when parents are involved in the process. In fact, John Goodlad noted that all the high achieving schools in his research sample could easily point to involved, informed parents; and for all the low-achieving schools parents seemed to be uninvolved and uninformed. Surprisingly, some of the high-achieving, high-parent-involvement schools were in poverty-stricken areas. He noted one high achieving school where the average formal education level of the parents was 4th grade (Goodlad, 1992). Parent involvement can cause difficulties, as we note later, but it is worth the effort and risks. When parents are involved in the process, schools will focus more on learning, and less on the social and political agendas that have dominated American education for the past several decades.

Our literature review on parental involvement indicates that there are few who question the importance of the role of parents in the education of the child. But what is meant by "involvement" takes different forms, and educators are not in agreement on the extent or scope to which parents should be involved. Joyce Epstein of Johns Hopkins University has spent considerable time studying the ways in which parents are involved in education and the schools. Her findings are presented in Figure 9.1. Each of these areas presents challenges to schools and parents. From these challenges, schools have designed a number of programs to increase meaningful parental involvement. There are literally hundreds of such programs around the country.

A useful resource for those who wish to consider such programs is *Innovations In Parent & Family Involvement*, by William Rioux and Nancy Berla (1993). Rioux and Berla describe in detail over 30 successful parental involvement programs, from elementary through high school, around the country. They furnish the reader with program evaluation and research information. A brief synopsis of a few of those programs is provided in Figure 9.2.

A number of researchers have articulated various components of parental involvement programs that seem to enhance the opportunities for success. These can serve as important guidelines as you consider beginning a parent invol-

FIGURE 9.1. FIVE MAJOR TYPES OF PARENT INVOLVEMENT

Type 1. *The basic obligations of parents* refers to the responsibilities of families to ensure children's health and safety; to the parent and child-rearing skills needed to prepare children for school; to the continual need to supervise, discipline, and guide children at each age level; and to the need to build *positive home conditions* that support school learning and behavior appropriate for each grade level.

Type 2. *The basic obligations of schools* refers to the *communications from school to home* about school programs and children's progress. Schools vary the form and frequency of communications such as memos, notices, report cards, and conferences, and greatly affect whether the information about school programs and children's progress can be understood by all parents.

Type 3. *Parent involvement at school* refers to parent *volunteers* who assist teachers, administrators, and children in classrooms or in other areas of the school. It also refers to parents who come to school to support student performances, sports, or other events, or to attend workshops or other programs for their own education or training.

Type 4. *Parent Involvement in learning activities at home* refers to parent-initiated activities or child-initiated requests for help, and ideas or instructions from teachers for parents to monitor or *assist their own children* at home on learning activities that are coordinated with the children's classwork.

Type 5. *Parent involvement in governance and advocacy* refers to parents' taking *decisionmaking* roles in the PTA/PTO, advisory councils, or other committees or groups at the school, district, or state level. It also refers to parent and community *activists* in independent advocacy groups that monitor the schools and work for school improvement.

Source: Brandt, R. (1989). "On Parents and Schools: A Conversation with Joyce Epstein." *Educational Leadership*, 47(2), p. 25.

vement program. We have summarized those findings and the recommendations of two of those writers in Figure 9.3.

FIGURE 9.2. TYPICAL PARENTAL INVOLVEMENT PROGRAM COMPONENTS

Elementary

Attenville Elementary School *Harts, WV*	Family center, parent phone tree, parent workshops, home visits, tutoring centers, welcome wagon
Balboa Elementary *San Diego, CA*	Parent institute training course, parent room, parent coordinator, governance team
Rockaway New School *Rockaway Beach, NY*	Parent volunteers, open and accessible classrooms, steering committee, parent meetings

Middle School

Crossroads School *New York, NY*	Advisory system, parent conferences, building bridges, "conversations" with parents, work parties
Morningside Middle School *Fort Worth, TX*	Parent visitation, parent discussion sessions, parent action committees

High School

Manual High School *Denver, CO*	Parent involvement requirements, orientation workshops, parents spend one day at school, incentives for parent involvement
Paul Robeson High School *Chicago, IL*	Annual retreat, adult learning, mentoring program, local school council, super parents group

---

Source: Rioux, J.W., & Berla, N. (1993). *Innovations In Parent & Family Involvement*. Princeton Junction, NJ: Eye on Education.

FIGURE 9.3. SUGGESTED GUIDELINES FOR PARENT INVOLVEMENT PROGRAMS

A. Seven Essential Elements

1. *Written policies* that legitimize the importance of parent involvement, help frame the context for program activities, and help insure that parent involvement is central to the school program.

2. *Administrative support* for insuring funds, meeting space, communication equipment, and human resources needed for program implementation.

3. *Training* for both staff and parents on developing partnering skills.

4. *Partnership approach* reflecting activities such as joint planning, goal setting, definitions of roles, program assessment, and school support efforts.

5. *Two-way communication* between home and school which occur frequently and on a regular basis.

6. *Networking* with other programs to share information, resources, and technical expertise.

7. *Evaluation* activities at key stages as well as at the conclusion of a cycle or phase that enable parents and staff to make programs revisions as needed.

Source: Adapted from Williams, D.L., & Chavkin, N.F. (1989). "Essential Elements of Strong Parent Involvement Programs." *Educational Leadership, 47*(2), pp. 18–20.

B. Guidelines for Meaningful Parent Involvement

1. Be both open minded and well-organized when engaging parent participation.

2. Offer parents a variety of roles in the context of a well-organized and long lasting program. Parents need to be able to choose from a range of activities which accommodate different schedules, preferences, and capabilities.

3. Communicate regularly to parents their importance in the

school success of their child.

4. Encourage parent involvement from the time children first enter school.

5. Teach parents that activities such as modeling reading behavior and reading to their children increase children's interest.

6. Develop parent programs that include a focus on parent involvement in instruction, assisting with homework, and monitoring the learning activities of older students.

7. Provide training for parents but remember that intensive, long-lasting training is neither necessary nor feasible.

8. Make an extra effort to involve the parents of disadvantaged students.

Source: Adapted from Cotton, K., & Wikelund, K.R. (1989). *Parent Involvement in Education*. Portland, OR: Northwest Regional Educational Laboratory, pp. 6–7.

Williams and Chavkin (1989) point to the need for a formal process of parent involvement. This wise suggestion minimizes the potential for misunderstanding of roles, something that inevitably arises in less structured circumstances. Another point they make relates to the need for training, not only for parents, but for *faculty* as well. To develop useful partnerships is not an easy task. And, of course, they point to the need to evaluate what happens, not merely as the end of obvious cycles of involvement, but in process as well. Cotton and Wikelund (1989) offer a number of helpful suggestions paramount among which, in our opinion, are early involvement and involvement in instruction.

EVALUATING PARENTAL INVOLVEMENT

POTENTIAL AND PITFALLS

The introductory comments to this chapter make it clear that we believe that the parent involvement movement in schools is a positive development. We are convinced that it can lead to the deeper participation of parents in the *education* of their children. The potential is there for true fundamental reform of *education*, not just bureaucratic reform of the schools.

Any professional knows about the problems that can develop when parents become involved in the schools. The threat to professional educators when "nonprofessionals" enter their domain and attempt to influence school activities and direction is easily understood. In Chicago, for example, parents and community members who make up the Local School Council for each school have a great deal to say about hiring and firing school administrators and teachers (1993). The implications of this empowerment are at once encouraging and staggering.

Sometimes the conflicts that develop when parents and professionals attempt to work together can be brutal. Indeed, the newspaper and television stories of conflict between school professionals and parents or parent groups serve as a reminder that much is at stake. Parents often approach issues as matters of their perception of the welfare of their individual children, while teachers and administrators are likely to see such challenges as threats to their professional judgment.

Such a situation in New York state was reported in the National Edition of the *New York Times* in November of 1993. The conflict began when a group of parents who were invited by the school to monitor their children's school work began to question the use of a whole language literature program and its corresponding teaching techniques. The result of the ensuing brouhaha was that the school principal was "banished to the district office and assigned clerical chores" until a hearing panel could decide whether she should be dismissed. The acrimonious series of events that led to this outcome came about, rightly or wrongly, because parents were involved. The *Times* article stated: "The conflict . . . can serve as a caution to those who view parental involvement in decisionmaking as an educational cure-all."

These stories will become more, not less, common as parent involvement increases. Some discover that what is going on in the name education is not particularly to their liking. Areas fraught with eminent peril include whole language, cooperative learning, and curricular concerns such as multicultural education, AIDS education, and social/political agendas such as inclusion and racial balance. Of course, these conflicts are inevitable, and it is our opinion that sincere, well-thoughtout attempts to involve parents will in fact minimize them. Attempts to keep parents out of the loop results, as we have noted, in lower achievement and greater potential dissension.

Depending on your perspective, these challenges to the public school agenda and *its modus operandi* may be a good or bad thing. But it has become increasingly clear that the schools are going to have to listen to parents and consider their perspectives or things will only get worse. Schools are not institutions that should respond to every whim of a society, but they must be accountable to some degree, and must represent the values which supports them both financially and morally. A common charge is that the American middle class is abandoning the public schools. But one might argue as well that the public schools have abandoned the middle class by turning away from traditional learning and the values of discipline, hard work, and high expectations, in favor of educational fads and values that reflect a social agenda and a social reconstructionist view of education.

EDUCATIONAL RESEARCH ON PARENTAL INVOLVEMENT

In the many years we have been in education we have never heard a reasonable challenge to the belief that the parents should be actively involved in their children's education. And the educational research wholeheartedly supports that contention. Individual studies, reviews of research, and government reports all support parent involvement.

The idea of parent involvement in the education of their children is an inherently practical idea, one that hardly needs a great deal of theoretical underpinning. Nevertheless, we would encourage you to read William Bennett's *List of Leading Cultural Indicators* (1993). Bennett uses U.S. government statistics to illustrate the importance of family structure and support not just in education but in life in general.

The Level 2 and Level 3 research in this area is impressive. Because of the nature of the programs and the research done, the two levels overlap considerably, and, therefore, we discuss them together. The research consists of experimental studies, program evaluations, and also a large number of other types of research, including correlational and causal-comparative studies. The list could seem endless, and we have included key references in the bibliography, but we will mention just a few important studies that represent the virtual agreement of all in education about the importance of parents in the education of their children.

Herbert Walberg has spent much of his career identifying the factors that influence learning. By examining thousands of research studies over the years, he has reached several generalized conclusions. His widely quoted article, "Improving the Productivity of America's Schools (1984) ," and his Educational Productivity Theory specify nine factors that influence student learning, and one of these nine factors is the importance of the home. This work was followed by a synthesis of research (Wang, Haertel, & Walberg, 1993) and an article titled, "What Helps Students Learn" (Wang, Haertel, & Walberg, 1993–94). In this work, Walberg and his colleagues analyzed 11,000 statistical findings which showed, "the most significant influences on learning (p. 74)." Of the 28 factors identified and their relative influences on learning, the home environment/parental support was number 4, just behind classroom management, metacognitive processes, and cognitive processes. Specifics in this home environment/parental support area included such variables as "Parental involvement in ensuring completion of homework" and "Parental involvement in improvement and operation of instructional programs." Walberg, *et. al.*, concluded:

> The category home environment/parental support was among the most influential of the 28 categories. The benefits of family involvement in improving students' academic performance have been well-documented, as have its effects on improving school attendance and on reducing delinquency, pregnancies, and dropping out (p. 77).

Research conducted on attempts at parent involvement has demonstrated the efficacy of such programs time and again. For example, Cotton and Wikelund (1989, p. 2) concluded:

The research overwhelmingly demonstrates that parent involvement in children's learning is positively related to achievement. Further, the research shows that the more intensively parents are involved in their children's learning, the more beneficial are the achievement effects. This holds true for all types of parent involvement in children's learning and for all types of ages of students.

Other types of research offer similar conclusions. Years of effective schooling research, that is, research designed to determine why some schools are more effective than others, has shown that schools are generally more effective when there is an emphasis on parent and community involvement. Specific variables that emerge from the research as important include consistent and effective communication with parents, special efforts to involve the parents of disadvantaged students, and parents becoming involved in the instructional program (Northwest Regional Educational Laboratory, 1990).

And so our review of this field leads us to the conclusion that the evidence is overwhelming and irrefutable—*parent involvement is crucial*. The research is diverse and conclusive. Administrators and teachers need to do everything in their power to get parents across the school (and, more importantly, across the education) threshold.

REFERENCES

Bennett, W. (1993). *List of Leading Cultural Indicators.*

Chicago Public Schools, Office of Reform (1993). *LSC Sourcebook: Basics for the Local School Council.* Chicago, IL: Board of Education of the City of Chicago.

Cotton, K., & Wikelund, K.R. (1989). *Parent Involvement in Education.* Portland, OR: Northwest Regional Educational Laboratory.

Goodlad, J. (1992). *Video taped interview with Arthur Ellis.* Seattle, WA: The International Center for Curriculum Studies, Seattle Pacific University.

Heyns, B. (1978). *Summer Learning and the Effects of Schooling.* New York: Academic Press. Cited in Stark, R. (1985). *Sociology.* Belmont, CA: Wadsworth Publishing.

Northwest Regional Educational Laboratory (1990). *Effective Schooling Practices: A Research Synthesis 1990 Update* (1990). Portland, OR: Northwest Regional Educational Laboratory.

Rioux, J.W., & Berla, N. (1993). *Innovations in Parent & Family Involvement*. Princeton Junction, NJ: Eye on Education.

Stevenson, H. (1992). Learning from Asian schools. *Scientific American, 267*(6), 70–76.

Walberg, H. (1984). Improving the productivity of America's schools. *Educational Leadership, 41*(8), 19–27.

Wang, M.C., Haertel, G.D., & Walberg, J.H. (1993). Toward a knowledge base for school learning. *Review of Educational Research, 63*(3), 249–94.

Wang, M.C., Haertel, G.D., & Walberg, J.H. (1993–94). What helps students learn? *Educational Leadership, 51*(4), 74–79.

Williams, D.L., & Chavkin, N.F. (1989). Essential elements of strong parent involvement programs. *Educational Leadership, 47*(2), 18–20.

Young, R.E. (1990). *A Critical Theory of Education: Habermas and Our Children's Future*. New York: Teacher's College Press.

10

EDUCATIONAL CHOICE

School choice has emerged as the major educational reform
issue of the Nineties.

John M. Strate & Carter A. Wilson

Maybe it is time to see how our public schools perform
against private schools and parochial schools.

Maryland Governor William Donald Schaefer

It [choice] will fragmentize ambition, so that the individual
parent will be forced to claw and scramble for the good of
her kid and her kid only, at whatever cost to everybody else.

Jonathan Kozol

I don't understand all the hoopla over school choice. Maybe
I'm missing something but I just can't see that it will be such
a panacea.

Jack Hamilton, Assistant Superintendent

It is difficult to get a man to understand something when his
salary depends upon his not understanding it.

Upton Sinclair

WHAT IS EDUCATIONAL CHOICE?

Of all the restructuring trends in American education today, none threaten the educational bureaucracy more than the drive for educational choice. And on no topic is the debate more vociferous and full of rancor. Simply put, educational choice means allowing parents to decide where they send their children to school. One might argue that this has always been possible. And so it has for some. The difference this time around is that the choices the wealthy have always had at their disposal will, to a certain degree, be extended to all. The whole matter becomes quite intriguing when it comes to defining what might be implied by the term "to a certain degree." As usual, public money is at stake so the stakes are high. As matters now stand, parents who have the money can send their children to public school or, if they pay tuition, to private school. Even in this case, public money is involved because private schools are tax exempt organizations, and thus are given de facto support by the state.

In the past decade the choice movement has expanded beyond the realm of those few who could afford private school tuition. In an attempt to keep the choice movement contained, many districts and states allow parents to select from the entire menu of public schools. In Idaho, Nebraska, Ohio, Utah,

Washington, Minnesota, Arkansas, and Iowa, for example, a student can theoretically attend any public school in the entire state. We say theoretically because the logistics might be difficult when it comes to transportation, but taxpayers can deduct transportation costs, for example, from their Minnesota state income tax. Tuition, transportation, book, etc., costs incurred in sending children to private schools are also tax deductible in Minnesota. The main point we wish to make here is that a parent who desires to send his/her child to a public school outside the normal attendance area of that child is free to do so.

Another facet of the choice movement is the small but growing home school movement. Statistics in this realm are not easily documented, but it appears that about 1% of the children in America are currently being home schooled. In recognition of the fact that home schooling does not seem to be a phenomenon that will dry up and blow away, states and districts are beginning to cooperate with home school parents, allowing them access to special facilities and services such as athletics, music, remedial help, etc.

These things are already happening and appear to be more and more taken for granted. The big issue is that of some type of support in the form of vouchers or tuition tax credits. As we mentioned earlier, tuition tax credits to parents who send their children to private (church-related or secular) schools are already in place in Minnesota. The constitutionality of the Minnesota law was upheld by the 1983 United States Supreme Court decision in *Mueller vs. Allen*. The Court ruled that tax deductions for "tuition, textbooks, and transportation" are indeed legal, making it possible for states to provide indirect support to private schools.

Tuition tax credits are one thing, vouchers another. In order to receive tuition tax credits, one must have a certain level of income for the idea of tax credits to be meaningful. Thus, the poor and the lower middle class derive little benefit from them. Still, *Mueller vs. Allen* sets a precedent of state contribution, however indirect, to school choice. It also sets a precedent for public schools to charge tuition to students who live outside a given school district.

Under a voucher plan, parents would receive a certain sum

which they could then apply toward tuition costs at any school, private or public. The Level 1 research, or theoretical basis, comes from the work of Nobel Prize winning economist Milton Friedman, who first suggested the idea in the 1950s. As a free market economist, Friedman theorized that the poor quality of the public schools could be traced to a lack of competition. He argued that impoverished parents and their children, in particular, are often trapped in schools of low quality because they cannot afford simply to pack up and move to the suburbs. Vouchers would empower poor parents to pay for the schools of their choice, private or public. Two things are worthy of note here. First is the fact that Friedman saw the coming school crisis decades before others did and his voucher plan is now more than 40 years old. Second, he argued early on against the position that vouchers would primarily benefit the upper and middle classes who would have more insight into how to use them.

More recently, John Chubb and Terry Moe argue in their book, *Politics, Markets and America's Schools* (1990), that a major obstacle to student achievement is the bureaucratic nature of school systems. Chubb and Moe maintain that such bureaucracies inhibit the professional expertise and judgment of principals and teachers, denying them the flexibility they need to get the job done in the classroom. The larger the system, the more intricate and frustrating is the bureaucratic structure. Principals and teachers, regardless of their position on vouchers, will tell anyone who will listen that red tape in the form of meetings, memos, directives, and legal constraints tends to have a depleting effect on their creativity and energy. Both Friedman and Chubb and Moe imply that one way to improve public schools is to make them compete with private schools for students.

There are those in America today who feel that the time has come to end the near monopoly that is American K-12 public education. The choice movement is an attempt to do just that. And there are those who firmly believe that the choice movement, if it reaches the stage of vouchers, will sound the death knell of Horace Mann's dream of the democratic common school movement in America. We will look at the arguments for and against choice, the four major types of choice plans, and the types of schools that are emerging to provide alternatives for parents and students.

THE BIG DEBATE

An important cultural value of American life is the freedom to make choices about the important elements of our lives. We choose where we want to live, where we want to work, which church we go to, which doctor to see when we are sick, and which mechanic we take our car to when it isn't working properly. It seems that for life's important dimensions there are a variety of options available. Those options are encouraged because of the belief that personal choice and the competition that flows from choice represent the best way to build effective institutions to serve the very diverse needs of our society. However, for some particular reason, this degree of choice has been discouraged in the K-12 school system. For this most important element of our lives, the education of our children, many parents feel they have little choice indeed.

For as long a time as any of us can remember, the public schools have had a near monopoly on the education of American children. This is not the case in most of the developed countries. By dictating what schools they will attend, and, therefore, what they will learn and how they will learn it, the state has prohibited parents and their children from exercising freedom of educational choice. The exception to this rule are the 12% of students who attend private schools and the estimated 1% who are home schooled. The absence of parental choice within the public school framework reached its zenith during the era of enforced busing designed to meet racial quotas. In the Seattle, Washington, Public Schools, a rather typical urban example, parents were requested to list their first five choices of school and were told they would probably get one of them. Busing, the opposite of choice, appears headed for extinction; but for the parents of young children who were daily required to ride a bus for an hour each way the memories die hard.

American Federation of Teachers President Albert Shanker has called our public school system the nearest thing we have to a Soviet-style state monopoly. The near-monopoly approach to public education has developed in spite of the great success of our "other" much less centralized educational system, that of higher education. It is generally considered to be the best in the world. Higher education in the United States is a loosely configured network of seemingly endless choices—vocational schools, 2-year colleges, regional colleges and universities, world-renowned research universities—all with differing curricula and environments in which to learn, both traditional and nontraditional. And among each of these types of institutions are a large number of private schools from which a student may choose, and from which students may receive aid in the form of government grants, loans, and scholarships. Rather than weakening or destroying the public sector, the competition from these private institutions appears to have made the state colleges and universities stronger and more accountable to the public. Also, the freedom of choice that students have to decide among the public institutions has also resulted in the same responsiveness.

It is useful to consider what other countries have attempted in the name of educational choice. Most of our counterparts currently permit much wider latitude to parents and children than we do. Our travels have taken us to Hong Kong, Russia, England, Ukraine, the Netherlands, Belgium, France, etc., where the blurring of church-state boundaries to support choice across the public-private spectrum is taken for granted.

In the Netherlands, for example, the Dutch Freedom of Education Act stipulates that "public-authority and private schools must be treated equally with regard to funding." This means that parents may make their choice of any of several types of private schools or public school and that there is no difference in expense incurred by the parent. Teacher salaries, equipment, etc., are paid for by government funds regardless of whether a school is public, church-related, or otherwise private. The precedent, but not the practice, for this exists in the United States in the form of the doctrine called "child-benefit" theory. In a 1930 U.S. Supreme Court decision (*Cochran vs. Louisiana State Board of Education*), it was ruled that state funds may be used to support learning in private, church-related schools so long as the primary benefit was to the child's education. In the Netherlands and many other countries it is considered to directly benefit the child when he or she is sent to the school of his or her parents' choice. We cite these examples not so much to build a case for choice across public-private lines as to show that precedent exists for doing so in democratic nations.

The debate over choice for the K-12 schools is charged with feeling. Politics have played a large part in the debate. Conservatives generally favor expanded, and even unlimited, choice. Liberals, on the other hand, see choice as a means to establish policies that will further divide the system into haves and have nots, as wealthier, more politically astute families take advantage of the options to flee the urban schools, thereby further reducing the effectiveness of the schools left to the poor and minorities. Somewhere in the midst of this vast matrix one finds the educational bureaucracies and teachers unions who see a clear and present danger to their hegemony. As though the issue were not confusing enough in terms of what the public wants, in 1993 a voucher-type plan placed before the voters of California was resoundingly defeated. Still, polls show that the choice movement is gaining ground, and it is sure to appear on ballot after ballot from state to state in the near future.

The educational literature of recent years has documented the debate fully (*e.g.,* Glazier, 1993; Bastian, 1992; Corwin, 1992; Hayes, 1992; Coons & Sugarman, 1991). It appears that the educational establishment has agreed (or been forced to respond) to develop a range of choices within the public sector. It is not uncommon for districts to offer students a range of different emphases from school to school. Almost any district of some size, for example, has an "alternative" high school. In spite of these far-ranging concessions, the clamor continues to allow the private sector to become a player in the options picture through the vehicle of vouchers. How that should be done and whether it is in our best interest to do so remains a topic of debate. Table 10.1 offers the reader the most typical "pros" and "cons" in this ongoing argument.

One of the most influential proponents of school choice is John Chubb of the Brookings Institute. In *Politics, Markets, and America's Schools* (1990), Chubb and Terry Moe report the results of a longitudinal study of public and private education

TABLE 10.1. PRIVATE SCHOOL CHOICE—PRO AND CON

Pro	Con
1. Monopoly of the public sector will be broken and competition will improve the public schools.	1. Public money to private schools will drain resources from public schools and reduce the quality.
2. Choice enhances the power and involvement of parents in the educational process.	2. Education is a public good and should be controlled by the public democratic process.
3. Choice will help to reduce bureaucracy and waste in education.	3. Consistency in regulation of schools is needed for quality reasons.
4. Choice will help to meet the needs of individual students.	4. Choice will not aid the lower social economic classes and will promote inequalities.
5. Choice will help to eliminate the deleterious effects of politics in education.	5. Choice programs will encourage private and charter schools of dubious quality.
6. Educational choice is a matter of personal liberty and therefore should be a priority of the government.	6. Public money to private, religious schools violates the principle of separation of church and state.
	7. Choice will allow society to evade its responsibility for education for the masses.

which concludes that school organization is one of the four major factors (along with socioeconomic status of the family, and socioeconomic status of the student body, and student ability) affecting student achievement. Their conclusion is to make all schools autonomous with regard to organization, creating a situation akin to market conditions and thus allowing the consumer to shop where he or she chooses.

Jonathan Kozol (1992a; 1992b), author of *Savage Inequalities* (1991), charges that choice plans are undemocratic. He takes a point of view diametrically opposed to that espoused by Chubb and Moe. Kozol (1992a, p. 90) states:

> . . . The idea behind choice (within a district), basically, is that if you let people choose, everybody will get the school they want. Everybody will have an equally free choice; everybody will have equal access. And, those I hear defend choice say it will not increase class or racial segregation. In fact, in virtually every case that I have seen, none of these conditions is met. People very seldom have equal choices, and even when they theoretically have equal choices, they rarely have equal access.

Kozol opposes all forms of choice. He foresees that the problems will become even greater when cross-district choice and voucher plans for private schools are enacted. He maintains that in all forms of choice, the poor and illiterate will suffer disproportionately and the rich will benefit. In his words, "People can't choose things they've never heard of. . . ." His point, of course, is that choice will benefit only the well-informed and well-connected, handicapping the poor even more than presently.

Exactly what is meant by the term "choice" is one of the reasons why the debate has been so heated. Choice conjures up many things to many people. Choice can mean anything from schools-within-schools in the public sector, a position favored by researcher John Goodlad (1992), to voucher plans designed to remove all barriers between public and private schools. The latter end of our imaginary continuum is, of course, more threatening to the established order of things. Schools-within-schools are well underway in districts around the country, so in that limited sense, the choice movement is no longer hypothetical. Cross-district choice plans in the form of magnet schools designed to draw students to more specialized curricular emphases, are up and running. In a number of states students are allowed to attend schools outside their home districts, and, in some cases, they can even enroll early in certain state college or university courses. The more radical end of the movement continues to make its case for expanding choice into the private sector through vouchers and/or tuition tax credits. At this stage, however, it hasn't happened on any widespread basis. Our guess for the long-term, however, is that it probably will. An outline of the various plans for choice are presented in Figure 10.1.

What kind of schools are available from which parents can choose? If choice becomes more and more acceptable, as we think it will, alternative forms of district organization and schooling will only increase. The types of schools presented in Figure 10.2 illustrate the range of thought which includes neighborhood schools, schools-within-schools, magnet schools, charter schools, and private schools. One could, of course, add home schooling to this list of parental options.

Of the various choice plans and types of schools identified in Figures 10.1 and 10.2, the most far ranging are the cries for deregulation of schools that involve the voucher or tax credit plans and the charter schools movement. In the aftermath of the bitterly contested 1993 California vote that overwhelmingly defeated a bill to allow tax dollars to be used to pay tuition at private schools, proponents promised that this is only the beginning of the fight.

A telling example is cited by Patricia Farnan (1993) who has worked with private sources to raise money for half-tuition vouchers for poor inner city students to attend private schools. According to Farnan, the response on the part of the parents was overwhelming, in spite of the fact they would have to somehow come up with the remainder of the tuition money

---

FIGURE 10.1. MAJOR APPROACHES TO SCHOOL CHOICE

---

1. *Within District Plans* involve a single school district offering parents a range of choices beyond neighborhood schools, ranging from selection of alternative and magnet schools to elimination of mandatory neighborhood schools.

2. *Cross-District Plans* or interdistrict plans give parents the option of selecting schools in a nearby district. The least costly and most innocuous way of proving this choice option is to allow schools, at their discretion, to accept a limited number of transfer students from other school districts. However, if only a few transfer students are accepted, this approach would circumvent choice and leave the present system unchanged.

3. *Statewide Plans* allow parents to select for their children any school in the state, including postsecondary institutions. While a few states have adopted such plans, the plans have not resulted in wide usage or transfer of students.

4. *Voucher or Tax Credit Plans* provide direct payment to private schools by the government for each student, or reimbursement, either through reduced tax bills or increased refunds, to parents choosing private or parochial schools. These plans have enjoyed little public support and no legislative success.

Source: Adapted from Strate, J.M., & Wilson, C.A. (1991). *Schools of Choice in the Detroit Metropolitan Area.* Detroit: Wayne State University.

---

themselves. In Farnan's words: "It is a horrible indictment of public education that so many low-income parents will make the half-tuition sacrifice (p. 25)." So we can only imagine that this fight will continue. Figure 10.2 outlines the alternatives in choice plans.

Only slightly less heated are the arguments over charter schools. This movement represents an attempt to deregulate and decentralize the educational process by turning a school over to virtually any group of people with legitimate interests in education. Under an agreement reached by contract or charter, the group must provide the education for the child. The

---

FIGURE 10.2. SCHOOL ALTERNATIVES IN VARIOUS CHOICE PLANS

◆ *Neighborhood Schools* are the schools located in a particular neighborhood and to which children are assigned because of proximity to their homes. While some neighborhood schools have unique features, most follow traditional curriculum and methods of instruction. Some choice plans allow movement between neighborhood schools on a space-available basis.

◆ *Schools-Within-Schools* are autonomous specialized programs that exist within a particular school building. For example, in one high school building there may be a traditional high school curriculum and program which serves the majority of the students, while also within the same building is a separate program with a special academic and vocational emphasis for those students interested in computers and technology, with their own curriculum, teachers, and schedule. In some schools there may actually be four or five "schools" within that school building, each with its own focus. The choice for the student and parents is to decide which of the "schools" the student will enter. This model allows for choice, while still assigning students to a neighborhood school, and increases alternatives when interdistrict movement is allowed.

◆ *Magnet Schools* are specially designed schools based on a certain educational philosophy, such as the theories of Maria Montessori, or with a special academic or vocational emphasis, such as science and technology, the fine arts, or foreign languages. In districts with choice, students may opt out of their assigned school to attend a particular magnet school within the district or, depending on the plan, neighboring districts or anywhere in the state.

◆ *Charter Schools* are the most controversial of the schools advocated by the public school choice proponents. Although there are a variety of models in different states, charter schools are operated under a contract between the local school board or state, and a particular group wanting to run the school, such as a group of teachers, cultural institutions, universities, or parents. The charter is generally good for 3 to 5 years, at which time it is reviewed to determine if the school is accomplishing its stated purpose in relation to student outcomes. Funding is provided by the state or district on a per student basis. Minnesota was the first state to approve such schools, but the movement is growing and charter schools have been approved by several other states, including Ohio and California.

◆ *Private Schools* receive no public funding support, receiving all income from private sources and tuition. Private education has always been an alternative to parents and students *if* a private school exists in a particular area, and *if* it can be afforded. The use of tax credits or vouchers to open this alternative to a wider range of families is, along with charter schools, one of the most controversial aspects of the educational choice movement.

---

charter for a school is granted by the district or state for a set period of time, usually 3 to 5 years, at which time it is evaluated. Presumably, if the student performance standards agreed to in the charter are met, the school will continue. If not, the charter will be revoked. Experiments with charter schools are currently under way in Milwaukee, Minneapolis, Boston, Baltimore, and other cities around the country. This phenomenon is definitely worth watching. Mulholland and Amsler (1992) provide the reader with a good description of charter schools (see Fig. 10.3). Another excellent reference is Sautter's work, *Charter Schools: A New Breed of Public Schools* (1993).

EVALUATING EDUCATIONAL CHOICE

POTENTIAL AND PITFALLS

The choice movement in education offers great promise for the fundamental reform of American education. If it moves to

FIGURE 10.3. WHAT ARE CHARTER SCHOOLS

- ◆ *Purpose*: To provide a truly different approach to schooling than what is already being offered in the public schools and designed to result in improved student learning outcomes through the use of innovative or different teaching methods, such as multiage classrooms. They are designed to establish new forms of accountability.

- ◆ *Organizer*: Individuals or groups, which may include teachers, parents, nonprofit social service agencies, and universities.

- ◆ *Sponsor*: State Department of Education, a local school board, and/or a special board organized to oversee the charter schools.

- ◆ *Charter School Contract*: Usually valid for 3 to 5 years and includes details on methods of instruction and forms of assessment to be used, how the school will comply with state requirements, and methods of accountability.

- ◆ *School Autonomy*: Truly decentralized and free from all normal district and state regulations, relying on site-based management teams.

- ◆ *Accountability*: Accountable to its sponsor as a public school, and the sponsor can revoke or renew the charter.

- ◆ *Funding*: Received directly from the state as do school districts, usually for the average amount spent in the state per student.

- ◆ *Admissions*: Can be limited by grade level, age, or specific population, such as at risk students. However, as a public school, charter schools cannot choose their students for specific qualities, such as ability or aptitude, nor discriminate in other ways.

Source: Adapted from Mulholland, L., & Amsler, M. (1992). *The Search for Choice in Public Education: The Emergence of Charter Schools.* San Francisco: Far West Laboratory for Educational Research and Development (ERIC Document Reproduction Service No. ED354583).

its logical conclusion, the educational bureaucracy will never be the same, and this alone is no doubt a good thing. The opening of the system to a wider range of players will present opportunities for innovators to reinvent school. Individual differences have long been recognized by educators, but schools look remarkably the same. Choice, competition, decentralization, and diversity are the pillars on which American higher education is built, and it is the envy of the world. There is no reason to think that those elements will not work for schools where students are under 18 years of age. The dividing line is arbitrary and should be removed. Additionally, it just seems to be the way things are going: for example, telephone companies, airlines, computers, mail service, and a host of other commercial enterprises have gone from monoliths to many competing companies, and the trend continues.

Telephone service presents the reader with a useful scenario when it comes to the matter of school choice and the extent to which schools ought to be deregulated. Only a few years ago there was *the* telephone company. Economists often cited it as an example of a good monopoly. Prices seemed reasonable and service was good. What more did the public want? And then, seemingly out of nowhere, the telephone company shattered into dozens of shards. Confusion seemed to reign. People didn't even know who their phone company was, and it might be different between local and long distance services. But despite all the confusion, market forces have came into play, making rates more competitive, unleashing the conditions for unparalleled creative advancements in the technology of telephone service.

Of course, schools and telephones are not the same thing. The seemingly inevitable march toward deregulation of the schools will bring with it a host of unforeseen and presently unknowable circumstances. There is the old saying, "If it isn't broken, don't fix it." More and more people seem to think it (education) just may be broken.

EDUCATIONAL RESEARCH AND CHOICE

Because the educational choice issue is a major policy question it really falls outside of the realm of educational researchers. At best it lends itself to *ex post facto* research where test scores from schools of choice might be compared to test scores from traditional schools of similar academic/social profiles. This has not proven to be a particularly satisfying line of inquiry because the differences seem always to outweigh the similarities in such comparisons. Nevertheless, it should be done wherever possible. Program and state evaluators may be able over time to determine if sites where choice was implemented benefited educationally in the form of higher test scores or other relevant variables. But this will be difficult to determine because isolating the choice variable from the complex matrix of school and home life is very difficult. The search for more useful lines of program evaluation research continues.

One area of research is worth noting. There is evidence from national opinion polls that the large majority of Americans favor educational choice (*e.g.*, Elam, 1990). This has also been supported by many local studies from around the country. We have tried to avoid extended quotes in this book, but we think the following one is particularly significant and a reasonable way to close this chapter.

In reviewing a major report on a recent public opinion survey in Detroit, Michigan, the director of the survey project, Michael J. Montgomery (Strate & Wilson, 1991) stated that he believed that the report was "probably the single most important document published in recent years on Detroit public education." In this project, the finding on public attitudes toward choice

> systematically refutes much of what we have been told about the prospects for adopting schools of choice as the predominant approach to improving public education in Detroit. Strate and Wilson found that Detroiters generally support school choice with blacks actually being more supportive than whites. Their findings contrast sharply with the claims of many Detroit education activists that there is widespread and intractable opposition to schools of choice throughout Detroit with particularly strong opposition in the black community.

Perhaps this anomaly is not surprising given that most of the discussion of the appropriateness of "choice" has heretofore taken place among a local education elite with clear stakes in the current system of essentially political governance of Detroit's schools. On the other hand, Strate and Wilson went around the usual suspects to gauge the opinion of the general public. Once there they found much deeper and more widespread support in Detroit for the market-oriented approach to education management inherent in schools of choice than even the movement's most committed supporters had expected to find (p. iii).

No other issue presented in this book has the potential to change education to the extent that the choice movement has. Far more than any of the others, it offers an alternative to bureaucratic restructuring and to the usual attempts to tinker with the system. If it goes forward changes will reach the foundation of the system, and they will be profound. Whether everyone will be pleased with the results is another question.

REFERENCES

Bastian, A. (1992). Which choice? Whose choice? *Clearing House,* *66*(2), 96–99.

Chubb, J.E., & Moe, T.M. (1990). *Politics, Markets, and America's Schools.* Washington, DC: The Brookings Institute.

Coons, J.E., & Sugarman, S.D. (1991). The private school option in systems of educational choice. *Educational Leadership,* *48*(4), 54–56.

Corwin, T.M. (1992). Introduction: Examining school choice issues. *Clearing House, 66*(2), 68–70.

Elam, S.M. (1990). The 22nd Annual Gallop Poll of the public's attitudes toward the public schools. *Phi Delta Kappan, 72*(1), 41–55.

Farnan, P. (1993). A choice for Etta Wallace. *Policy Review, 64* (2), 24–27.

Glazier, N. (1993). American public education: The relevance of choice. *Phi Delta Kappan, 74*(8), 647–50.

Goodlad, J. (1992). *Video taped interview with Arthur Ellis.* Seattle, WA: The International Center for Curriculum Studies, Seattle Pacific University.

Hayes, L. (1992) A simple matter of humanity: An interview with Jonathan Kozol. *Phi Delta Kappan, 74* (4), 334–37.

Kozol J. (1992a). I dislike the idea of choice, and I want to tell you why. *Educational Leadership, 50*(3), 90–92.

Kozol J. (1992b). Flaming folly. *Executive Educator, 14*(6), 14–19.

Kozol J. (1991). *Savage Inequalities: Children in America's Schools.* New York: Crown.

Mulholland, L., & Amsler, M. (1992). *The Search for Choice in Public Education: The Emergence of Charter Schools.* San Francisco: Far West Laboratory for Educational Research and Development (ERIC Document Reproduction Service No. ED354583).

Sautter, R.C. (1993). *Charter Schools: A New Breed of Public Schools.* Oakbrook, IL: North Central Regional Educational Laboratory.

Strate, J.M., & Wilson, C.A. (1991). *Schools of Choice in the Detroit Metropolitan Area.* Detroit: Center for Urban Studies, Wayne State University (ERIC Document Reproduction Service No. ED355287).

11

INSTRUCTIONAL GROUPING ALTERNATIVES

Given the antidemocratic nature of ability grouping and the absence of evidence that grouping is beneficial, it is hard to justify continuation of the practice. . . . Yet schools and districts moving toward heterogeneous grouping have little basis for expecting that abolishing ability grouping will in itself significantly accelerate student achievement unless they also undertake changes in curriculum or instruction that are likely to improve actual teaching.

Robert Slavin

Ability grouping has long been a controversial topic in American education. Researchers have been collecting data on its effect for almost three-quarters of a century and still disagree about its merits. . . . The central and overriding message in numerous reviews of grouping research is that nothing has been established with certainty.

James and Chen-Lin C. Kulik

Schools do not need more organization, they need more creativity. A schedule should enhance the learning process, not hinder it.

Robert Spear

The basic design of high schools and the assumptions that lie behind it are at the heart of the problem.

Theodore Sizer

WHAT ARE INSTRUCTIONAL GROUPING ALTERNATIVES?

As we have noted more than once in this book, few of these topics are new. Most of the proposed changes have been tried from time to time in some form. The current restructuring efforts which call for alternative ways to group students fit that description. They often overlap such efforts as school choice, cooperative learning, and integrated curriculum. We have chosen to examine various proposed changes separately in order to display their merits and faults in sharper relief. The focus in this chapter is on alternatives to traditional graded instruction and grouping in elementary and secondary schools.

INSTRUCTIONAL GROUPING ALTERNATIVES IN THE ELEMENTARY SCHOOL

The dominant organizational pattern in the vast majority of elementary schools during this century has been the grouping of children by age in classes of 25 to 30 students taught by one teacher who in general teaches the class the same curriculum. This arrangement has served more an administrative than a learning function, and in some ways it has been an efficient way to group students. Within each classroom, especially at primary levels, it has also been common for the teacher to divide students into groups and to differentiate instruction with concessions to perceived (high, medium, low) ability. In addition to this basic pattern, some schools provide separate classes for remedial and, occasionally, for advanced students. These classes range from all-day affairs to pull-out approaches.

While its durability says something for it, the age-graded classroom has been the object of continued attack over the years by concerned educators. Critics of this model have generally expressed two related concerns. The first objection is that there simply are no demonstrated principles of learning and/or growth and development undergirding age-related grouping. This is a serious charge because it implies that we have placed organizational contrivance ahead of children's needs. Almost anyone would say that learning is the primary purpose of school, so what does it say about us when we make organizational connivance our first priority?

The second objection is mainly about what happens *within* these age-graded classrooms, although it spills over to a concern with special classes as well. The issue here is the undemocratic nature of ability grouping. Students are labeled early on in reading groups as high, medium, and low readers. The intent may be benign, that is, to help students at their perceived skill level. But the effect, according to critics, is to create artificial feelings of inferiority and superiority. The feelings of inferiority may well outweigh the well-intentioned attempts at remediation. Who knows?

A range of alternative grouping procedures have been proposed over the years (see Fig. 11.1), and most of them are attempts to address one or both of the foregoing concerns. Ability grouping is currently under heavy fire, and even such minimal concessions to ability as the Joplin plan (see Fig. 11.1) are being questioned. The main idea seems to be to remove the stigma of group membership, whether low or high, and to place emphasis on the individual in a community of learners. This is far easier to talk about than to accomplish, but that is not a reason not to attempt it.

FIGURE 11.1. ELEMENTARY GROUPING ALTERNATIVES

Graded Classrooms refers to the traditional practice of grouping students by age and assigned a grade level. For example all 8-year-olds are placed in the 3rd grade, all 9-year-olds in the 4th grade, and so forth. Such classrooms are usually heterogeneous in terms of ability except perhaps for the most low-ability student.

Ability Grouping is the practice of grouping homogenous students for instruction. This grouping procedure may take place within a graded classroom, or may result in the placement of low or high ability students in special classrooms, resulting in a homogenous group of students. This practice may extend past the elementary school and into the middle schools and high schools.

Nongraded Education divides children into heterogeneous classes based on age and ability levels. Grade designations (not the letter grade associated with achievement) are removed from the curriculum, and a student passes through the curriculum at his or her own rate, typically staying with the same teacher for 2 or 3 years.

Joplin Plan is a system of instructional grouping in graded schools that regroups students, generally for part of the school day, on the basis of a single ability, irrespective of the grade level or age of the student. For example, all students in an elementary school who are reading at the 3rd grade level or below would go to a particular teacher's room for reading instruction only.

The major alternative grouping trend of the 1990s is nongraded education, variably called continuous progress, multiage grouping, vertical grouping, and multigrade grouping. In essence, its form is a heterogeneous collection of students of varying ages (usually with a range of 3 to 4 years) in a single classroom. The idea is that children will work at their own pace, being neither promoted or retained. Students are assessed against their own standards of success and with authentic assessment procedures (see Chapter 12). The curriculum and teaching goals of such an arrangement are based on what are thought to be developmentally appropriate activities and include both the academic and affective areas of a child's development. This model was proposed in 1959 (reissued in 1987) by John Goodlad and Robert Anderson in their book, *The Nongraded Elementary School.* A rationale for such a school structure is presented in Figure 11.2.

FIGURE 11.2. REASONS FOR NONGRADED PRIMARY EDUCATION

◆ Chronological age and mental age do not always correspond.

◆ Children are able to work at different developmental levels without obvious remediation, thus avoiding the social or emotional damage typically caused by retention.

◆ Students stay with their teacher for more than 1 year providing for continuity of learning.

◆ Age and achievement differences are accepted as normal by children.

◆ Nongraded arrangements lend themselves to integrated curriculum.

◆ The increasing diversity of contemporary society is more easily accommodated by nongraded programs.

◆ Nongraded grouping leads to more positive student attitudes and behavior, with no loss of academic achievement.

◆ Nongraded programs are more in keeping with the way children in naturalistic settings spontaneously group themselves for play and projects.

◆ Nongraded programs avoid many of the drawbacks of traditional practices, such as retention and acceleration issues.

Source: Adapted from Cotton, K. (1993). *Nongraded Primary Education.* Portland, OR: Northwest Regional Educational Laboratory.

INSTRUCTIONAL GROUPING ALTERNATIVES IN THE SECONDARY SCHOOL

Many issues related to grouping in elementary schools are also concerns at the secondary level, including middle, junior, and senior high schools. The questions associated with ability grouping are the same, but become even more complex as differences among students increase with age and while occupational and/or university preparation becomes more focused. Heterogeneous groupings or nontracked programs greatly intensify the issues, and everyone seems to agree that they present a challenge to meeting the needs, desires, and interests of all students.

The traditional departmentalized structure still dominant at most high schools appears to be slowly giving way to a variety of options, many of which are related to issues of educational choice (see Chapter 10). Some of the more common forms of organization are described in Figure 11.3, and, as is evident, many revolve around the perceived future needs of students as they move on either to higher education or into the job market. The arrangements themselves actually represent a rather creative range of options, but the concern won't die that some of them are just other ways to track by socioeconomic class, race, or gender. Americans feel very deeply about three values: equality, excellence, and personal choice. We want them all. But what happens when the values we so deeply cherish conflict with each other?

EVALUATING INSTRUCTIONAL GROUPING ALTERNATIVES

POTENTIAL AND PITFALLS

How to group students is an important consideration for schools, but as a single consideration it is simply bureaucratic restructuring. Whether regrouping students, particularly at the elementary level, will lead to fundamental changes in what and how students learn is problematic. The grouping of students becomes a meaningful issue only when it is considered within the matrix of community, individuals, and a coherent philosophy of moral judgments about teaching and learning.

FIGURE 11.3. SECONDARY GROUPING TERMINOLOGY

Departmentalized middle and high school programs are the traditional arrangements where students receive instruction in each content area from separate teachers.

Core blocks are lengthened periods of time, usually two to three class periods, where one teacher teaches the same group of students over two or more subject areas. It is more common at the middle school level, and very appropriate for an integrated curriculum.

Occupational clusters allow students to sample various occupational offerings depending on interest. In this model, traditional departments are often replaced and students can select a "major," and, therefore, multiple classes from the variety of occupational clusters.

Schools-within-schools are schools with either an academic or occupational focus. There may be two or more schools within a particular school building, and students are free to choose which "school" they enter. Sometimes called academies, they focus on a particular occupational or academic area, such as the health sciences, business, or the arts. They many times involve a cohort of students and a select number of teachers who stay together for 2 or 3 years. Learning is thematic and many times tied to community activities and involvement.

Copernican plan calls for longer class periods in the morning (up to 4 hours) and of shorter duration (30 days). Its intent is to allow students to deal with more complex issues and to take more credits during the year. It is also touted as a way to reduce teacher contact hours with students each day to allow for more planning and more opportunity to personalize instruction.

Magnet schools are specialty schools that emphasize an occupational area such as fashion, music and the arts, or science and technology. They are generally a separate high school and a part of the choice options available in some districts.

We are convinced on the basis of our experience and our review of the literature that how students are organized is a significant concern but not a place to begin the process of restructuring.

At the secondary level the issue is so closely associated with educational choice that it is hard to separate the two. Most of the programs outlined in Figure 11.3 have the potential to lead to true fundamental reform because (1) they do require an examination of the curriculum demanded by the programs, (2) they can truly lead to improved student attitudes about school and learning because of the choice element, and (3) they focus on student interest and planning for the future. These matters address the criticisms of the single-minded traditional curriculum and would constitute the beginning of the process of fundamental reform in secondary education.

There are potential pitfalls however, and we will mention three obvious ones. First, particularly at the elementary level, focusing great energies on grouping practices can distract from other reform components that may be more important than how students are grouped. When these energies are not directed by a clear goal-oriented/participatory perspective on reform, they become arbitrary. Second, simply instituting a nongraded arrangement, or ability groups, or large group instruction, or heterogeneous grouping, or a Joplin plan without corresponding training for teachers to teach in such an arrangement will accomplish little. Forces of inertia will emerge, and before you know it you're back to the old "tried and true" ways, and the cynics are able once more to say, "we told you so." Grouping patterns should be part of a larger overall strategy which includes concern for teachers, students, parents, and any others who will be affected.

Research (Miller, 1991) indicates that certain teacher skills of classroom management, classroom organization, instructional organization and curriculum, instructional delivery and grouping, self-directed learning, and peer tutoring are necessary before the nongraded classroom will be effective. A change to nongraded classes done in ignorance of these variables will probably be counterproductive.

At the secondary level, the fear that choice programs with emphases on academic and/or specific vocational directions will lead to the placement of disproportionate numbers of minorities and students of lower socioeconomic backgrounds into less "prestigious" or lower quality programs is legitimate in our opinion. Fear of tracking should not be a reason to avoid alternative grouping arrangements based on curricular levels or emphases, but equity issues are far from trivial. Whether particular arrangements are valid can only be answered reasonably on the basis of careful thought and decisionmaking by those who will be most affected.

EDUCATIONAL RESEARCH AND INSTRUCTIONAL GROUPING

Sorting out the research on the broad topic of grouping is difficult. The variety of questions which researchers have posed about ability groups, single- and multiple-age groups, partial day pull-out plans, and so forth, make the matter complex. For each of these topics, there are multiple combinations of questions that can be posed. We limit our examination of the research to three areas: (1) the effects of nongraded education; (2) the effects of ability grouping; and (3) the effects of secondary grouping practices.

NONGRADED EDUCATION

The Level 1 research for nongraded education is based in the belief of the importance of developmentally appropriate practices which have emerged from the work of child psychologists and developmental specialists. Advocates point to the seminal works of John Dewey, Maria Montessori, Jean Piaget, and others as providing the theoretical framework. Goodlad and Anderson's book, *The Nongraded Elementary School* (1959, 1987), provides any interested person with the range of theoretical to practical constructs undergirding this idea.

The Level 2 and Level 3 research is very much indistinguishable, so we discuss them together. The bottom line question for researchers is, and has been, how does student achievement compare between students who are in nongraded (multiage) classrooms with those who are in single-age graded classrooms. A second area of concern is with other educational outcomes, such as attitudes toward school, and social and emotional development. This is a not a new question, having been around for well over a century.

Rural schools have been a focus of these research efforts for many years, and folks living in the country have long wondered about it as more and more schools and districts have become consolidated and larger. Originally, the research focused on one- or two-room schools and was valuable to rural residents as they wondered whether to maintain their small schools and multiage classes, which were based not on a philosophy of schooling but on a preference for a simpler life.

There is a large body of research on this topic, but we must add that it is difficult research to do well because the single variable of grouping is difficult to isolate for cause and effect purposes. Common sense will tell you that grouping alone is never the single variable in any teaching/learning equation. Consequently, the research takes a variety of forms: causal-comparative, *ex post facto*, and program evaluation. Nevertheless, it has been conducted for many years and is instructive. A number of reviews of the research on grouping are available. We will give you a review of the reviews.

The research appears to lead to three conclusions. First, there are a number of researchers who conclude that the effect on academic achievement of nongraded grouping is inconclusive. Ansah (1989) concluded that some children seem to benefit from nongraded classes, while others seem to do better in single grade groups. Pratt (1986) found no consistent advantage of one grouping plan over another in academic achievement, as did Cotton (1993), Miller (1990; 1991), and Ford (1977). McGurk and Pimentle (1992) also found that academic achievement was comparable between nongraded and graded classroom, but did find empirical support for the Joplin Plan.

Second, there are a few researchers who conclude that children may do slightly better in nongraded classrooms (Pavan, 1977; 1992; Guitierrez & Slavin, 1992).

Third, there is general concurrence that "multiage grouping appears to offer some advantages in affective growth," particularly in the areas of attitude toward school, self-concept, self-esteem, aspirations, feelings of success, and perceptions of parental approval (Ford, 1977, p. 158)." Pratt (1986) and Miller (1990) say much the same thing. Cotton (1993, p. 6) concludes that "research overwhelmingly favors nongraded grouping because of its positive affects on" attitudes toward school, self-concept, classmates, self-esteem, anxiety future aspirations, social skill development, leadership skill development, frequency of interaction with other-age peers, prosocial behaviors and reduced aggression, attendance, retention, teacher-student interactions, and parent attitudes toward school. This is an impressive laundry list of accomplishments. Proponents of nongraded education can point to a long research base which shows that achievement is at least comparable to graded classes, and may be better. The strongest argument for change appears to come from findings in the affective areas.

ABILITY GROUPING

The research literature on ability grouping is both extensive and hotly debated. In fact, it's a real barn burner. We summarize as best we can what it says. We encourage you to seek out the many sources (Slavin, 1987; 1990; 1993; Hallinan, 1990; Kulik & Kulik, 1984; 1987; Kulik, 1991; Allan, 1991). It's fair to say that those who have reviewed the many studies on grouping students by ability are not in agreement on exactly what effect the practice has on achievement and self-esteem. Charges are made of poor methodology, misinterpretation of data, etc., and some maintain that the findings are being used inappropriately by well-meaning but biased educators to eliminate all types of grouping from the schools.

Such contradictory and confusing research findings exist, and such respected researchers disagree over the findings, that we believe that it appropriate to admit that the research is not clear at this point. In fact, this may be a topic that can never be researched in a manner that will satisfactorily and conclusively answer the question for all concerned. There is a good possibility that it may be virtually impossible to isolate the grouping effect as a single variable to show cause and effect. This problem may obtain more often than not in educational research, a problem that is not limited to studies of grouping. Perhaps how students are taught, for example, is as important as how they are grouped. Teaching method and grouping pattern are merely examples of variables in a list that could be greatly expanded. This leaves the door open for disagreement over educational research findings in almost any area you can imagine.

SECONDARY GROUPING PRACTICES

The ability grouping research and ensuing disagreements extend to the secondary level as well, but in this section we look at what is known about the types of secondary grouping mentioned in Figure 11.3.

Much of the effective schools research identifies an "affective" element of successful schools and teaching not found in less successful educational efforts. The effective schools research indicates that the affective environment of the schools and the classrooms are an important influence on measurable outcomes. While much of the research does not deal directly with the affective environment, it is implied throughout the findings. For example, research indicates that a pleasant, safe, personalized environment is important (Northwest Regional Educational Laboratory, 1990). Milbrey McLaughlin and Joan Talbert (1990) of Stanford University use the words, "family," "a climate of caring and respect," "intimacy," and "feeling valued," when describing these environments. The effective schools research shows that these environments enhance learning of traditional educational outcomes of an academic and intellectual nature. Students seem to learn more in caring, personalized environments. Certainly this is difficult to accomplish in large impersonal schools, and many of the regrouping efforts at the secondary level are attempts to overcome the impersonalized nature of the educational environment and curriculum.

At Levels 2 and 3 we have not found good quality published studies that show the efficacy of such arrangements. Such benign conditions in schools and classrooms are indeed compelling in their attractiveness, but this must remain a matter of conjecture since the research is not as solid as the folk wisdom at this point. Good evaluation research is desperately needed if we are to make meaningful restructuring decisions in this area.

References

Allan, S.D. (1991). Ability-grouping research reviews: What do they say about grouping and the gifted? *Educational Leadership, 48*(6), 60–65.

Ansah, V. (1989). *Multiage Grouping and Academic Achievement.* (ERIC Document Reproduction Service No. ED315163).

Cotton, K. (1993). *Nongraded Primary Education.* Portland, OR: Northwest Regional Educational Laboratory.

Ford, B.E. (1977). Multiage grouping in the elementary school and children's affective development: A review of recent research. *The Elementary School Journal, 78*(2), 149–59.

Goodlad, J.I., & Anderson, R.H. (1987). *The Nongraded Elementary School. Revised Edition.* New York: Teacher's College Press.

Guitierrez, R., & Slavin, R. (1992). Achievement effects of the nongraded elementary school: A best-evidence synthesis. *Review of Educational Research, 62*(4), 333–76.

Hallinan, M. (1990). The effects of ability grouping in secondary schools: A response to Slavin's best evidence synthesis. *Review of Educational Research, 60*(3), 501–04.

Kulik, J.A. (1991). Findings on grouping are often distorted. *Educational Leadership, 48*(6), 67.

Kulik, C.L., & Kulik, J.A. (1984). *Effects of Ability Grouping on Elementary School Pupils: A Meta-Analysis.* Paper presented at the 92nd Annual Meeting of the American Psychological Association, Aug. 24–28, 1984, Toronto, Canada (ERIC Document Reproduction Service No. ED255329).

Kulik, C.L., & Kulik, J.A. (1987). Effects of ability grouping on student achievement. *Equity and Excellence, 23*(1), 22–30.

McGurk, E.K., & Pimentle, J.A. (1992). *Alternative Instructional Grouping Practices.* (ERIC Document Reproduction Service No. ED353279).

McLaughlin, M.W., & Talbert, J. (1990). Constructing a personalized school environment. *Phi Delta Kappan, 72*(3), 230–35.

Miller, B.A. (1990). A review of the quantitative research on multigrade instruction. *Research in Rural Education, 7*(1), 1–8.

Miller, B.A. (1991). A review of the qualitative research on multigrade instruction. *Research in Rural Education, 7*(2), 3–12.

Northwest Regional Educational Laboratory (1990). *Effective Schooling Practices: A Research Synthesis 1990 Update* (1990). Portland, OR: Northwest Regional Educational Laboratory.

Pavan, B.N. (1992). The benefits of Nongraded Schools. *Educational Leadership, 50*(2), 22–25.

Pavan, B.N. (1977). The nongraded elementary school: research on academic achievement and mental health. *Texas Tech Journal of Education, 4*(2), 91–107.

Pratt, D. (1986). On the merits of multiage classrooms. Their work life. *Research in Rural Education, 3*(3), 111–16.

Slavin, R. (1987). Ability grouping and student achievement in elementary schools: A best-evidence synthesis. *Review of Educational Research, 57*(3), 293–336.

Slavin, R. (1990). Achievement effects of ability grouping in secondary schools: A best-evidence synthesis. *Review of Educational Research, 60*(3), 471–99.

Slavin, R. (1993). Ability grouping in the middle grades: achievement effects and alternatives. *Elementary School Journal, 93*(5), 535–52.

12

ALTERNATIVE ASSESSMENT

The only way to improve schools . . . is to ensure that
faculties judge local work using authentic standards and
measures. . . . It means doing away with the current extremes
of private, eccentric teacher grading, on the one hand, and
secure standardized tests composed of simplistic items on the
other.

Grant Wiggins

. . . Alternative assessment's rising tide has overflowed most
of education's shoreline, and the schools are increasingly
being flooded with calls for more direct assessment of
student performance. . . . Many practitioners are unsure
whether to venture into the torrents of unfamiliar assessment
strategies or to drift quietly in education's backwaters,
waiting to see if this movement crests and ebbs as quickly as
have dozens of others.

Blaine R. Worthen

What is Alternative Assessment?

Alternative assessment strategies have emerged as a key element of the school restructuring movement. Like so many of the varied pieces of the vast and often contradictory school restructuring puzzle, alternative assessment represents a frontal attack on the status quo. At the energizing source of the alternative assessment paradigm is a deep and abiding dissatisfaction with traditional evaluation procedures, both standardized tests and teacher-made achievement tests. But it doesn't stop there; the alternative assessment movement has produced a number of nontraditional ideas for taking into account student learning.

As one might expect, an entire range of terms and phrases has emerged. The significant vocabulary includes authentic assessment, performance assessment, practical testing, and direct testing. Whatever the terminology, the move to alternative assessment practices is reaching epic proportions. To place this movement into some kind of meaningful context, it is necessary to develop a contrasting image of more traditional assessment patterns and their effects on students.

WHAT DID YA GIT?

Student progress is traditionally assessed and reported along a feedback continuum which incorporates everything from daily marks to midterm grades to quarter and semester grades to standardized test scores. These marks take on a life of their own, creating a sense of reality in the minds of teachers, students, and parents. In fact, this "reality" may or may not have curriculum content validity; that is, the tests, and therefore the grades which flow from them, may or may not be very well-connected to the curriculum that is taught to students. There is, in fact, a long history of discontent with both standardized and teacher-made tests.

From another viewpoint, standardized tests furnish communities, districts, states, and the nation with benchmarks of comparative scores over time and with one another. Thus, we can compare any given district with its own past performance and with other districts; we can compare, for example, Vermont with Nevada. And so on. For all its perceived shortcomings, it is a relatively efficient system, one that has been around for at least 50 years. Still, the criticisms have become more and more strident and they cannot be ignored.

Thomas Toch takes standardized tests to task in his book, *In the Name of Excellence* (1991). He cites the many standardized tests that states have put in place as a means of holding teachers accountable. Thinking that such tests will lead to improved classroom performance because teachers will "know" that they have to prepare their students better, state legislators have enacted legislation requiring tests in the majority of the states. But Toch sees this as nothing more than a return to "minimum competency testing," a movement that was tried and failed in the 1970s. In a very thoughtful passage, Toch (p. 207) writes:

> Yet there is an immense paradox in the recent surge in standardized testing. Despite the key role standardized tests are playing in the reformers' accountability campaign, the bulk of the new tests are severely flawed as measures of the excellence movement's progress. One

major reason is that the tests do not measure the sorts of advanced skills and knowledge that the reformers have argued all students should master. . . . It is largely impossible to gauge from the results of such tests whether students are mastering the intellectual skills that have been the focus of the reform movement: the abilities to judge, analyze, infer, interpret, reason, and the like. Nor do the majority of the tests gauge students' more advanced knowledge of literature, history, science, and other disciplines. Indeed, the recent surge in standardized testing amounts to little more than an extension of the minimum basic-skills testing movement of the 1970s.

This very vexing problem carries with it yet another twist, as though the ongoing critique that standardized tests (and teacher-made tests as well) tend to measure only lower-register thinking and knowledge wasn't enough. In an article published in the *American Psychologist* in 1973, David McClelland, a noted researcher whom we definitely categorize as a Level 1 theoretician, criticized standardized testing in the most basic sense. He proposed teaching people how to raise their test scores, testing abilities rather than "aptitudes," designing tests so that people's scores would rise as they learned more, abandoning multiple choice formats, all of which is yet to happen. But his most fundamental suggestion for change was his idea that we need to stop ranking millions of people on their perceived knowledge and skills and start building tests that tap into people's motivations for learning, something that could actually be used to shape instruction for individuals (Lehman, 1994).

AUTHENTIC ASSESSMENT

Serious students of restructuring are committed to a review of the entire educational system, and this would certainly involve a close look not only at how we have traditionally evaluated students but on the effects on them of how they have been evaluated. Perhaps the key to understanding the alternative assessment movement is found in a thoughtful consideration of the term "authentic assessment." Authentic assessment implies that, by contrast, it should replace assessment that is inauthentic, a term which means false. The idea of authentic assessment is to create evaluation strategies that measure more realistically and accurately those things that students are supposed to be learning.

Students proceed through their school years being evaluated on daily, weekly, quarterly, etc., bases, taking teacher-made tests, doing assignments such as directed readings, reports, and projects. For this they receive semester or yearly marks, many times in the form of letter grades, sometimes supplemented by narrative teacher evaluations. In a (seemingly) unrelated process, once a year (sometimes less often), they take standardized tests in such basic skill areas as mathematics and reading, and in such content areas as social studies and science. These tests are at best variably connected to the curriculum that is actually taught at a given school. It is when the results are disappointing and they get in the newspapers that school people become so discouraged. In fact, a typical defensive reaction by teachers is that their students are learning many wonderful things but that those things are not effectively captured by the tests. Of course, when the results are good we all seem to take them for granted.

In a more perfect educational world (the goal of restructuring), it would be impossible to separate assessment procedures from curriculum content. If we are to do authentic assessment, it stands to reason that we should be assessing what is being taught and, one hopes, what is being learned. So, first of all, for assessment to be authentic it should be as closely aligned as possible to the day-to-day experiences of the curriculum. Here there really is little argument between traditionalists and those who would change the assessment paradigm. But good alignment is not enough. It's just a place to start.

Second, it is argued that teaching and learning should be authentic. This term means that learning should focus on real life situations. "Let students encounter and master situations that resemble real life (Cronin, 1993, p. 79)." The curricular implications of this view are clearly that school activities and projects should have a real-world cast to them. This argument has been around forever, and it basically represents a philosophic divide between those who espouse an academic-centered curriculum and those who espouse a more society-centered curriculum.

The Center on Organization and Restructuring of Schools at the University of Wisconsin at Madison, has developed a framework for "authentic instruction," and "authentic achievement" (Newmann and Wehlage, 1993). Newmann and Wehlage draw a distinction between "achievement that is significant and meaningful, and that which is trivial and useless." They use three criteria to define authentic achievement: "(1) students construct meaning and produce knowledge, (2) students use disciplined inquiry to construct meaning, and (3) students aim their work toward production of discourse, products, and performances that have value or meaning beyond success in school (p. 8)." We presume that experiences which do not meet these criteria are "trivial and useless."

Not all advocates of alternative assessment procedures have such definitively articulated ideas about achievement, but the essence of their argument is the same: what we teach and what we assess are not what is important for students to learn. All too often it is removed from the "real world" that students will face when they leave school. Therefore, they argue, it behooves us to rethink our assessment techniques, and, therefore, our curriculum, to provide and assess learning that is authentic, and not contrived. Such a statement presumes that school is not part of the real world.

The alternative assessment movement is obviously based on two related arguments, one which deals with curriculum and the other with assessment. First, is the ancient, abiding debate over the curriculum, and the relevance of school learning to the real world. The belief in such a dichotomy, of course, can serve as a self-fulfilling prophecy. The question becomes, does what students are taught in the schools apply to reality, that is, can they use their knowledge to solve problems, do their jobs, and lead their lives? Second, what do traditional evaluation strategies such as paper and pencil tests and standardized tests really measure, and whatever that is, is it important?

The proponents of alternative assessment strategies have

definite and predictable responses to these questions. School learning must be reality-based, and the assessment of that learning must be more natural, a logical outgrowth of the learning experiences themselves. Many of those who hope to restructure education agree and have joined the movement seeing it as crucial. There appear to be four reasons why alternative assessment is seen as a key to restructuring.

First, alternative assessment strategies are seen as educationally superior to traditional methods. The strategies call for more formative and personalized assessment for the individual student. To do this will provide meaningful feedback to the individual, thus creating the possibilities for more significant, useful learning. The focus shifts naturally to higher level thinking skills and real real-life applications that increase student interest and motivation.

A second line of reasoning is that alternative forms of assessment will provide a more adequate representation of what is actually being taught in the schools today. Current standardized tests lack validity as measures of the diverse curricular offerings. It's an interesting argument and one that has a certain elemental appeal, but the idea behind good standardized tests is that they capture students' ability to apply concepts and skills, not their narrowly-defined content data knowledge.

A third point is that authentic learning and alternative assessment strategies will facilitate the type of learning that is needed by employees to allow the United States to compete internationally. Here is an example. Students who use alternative assessment procedures are more involved in assessing their own learning and are, therefore, more aware of their learning. This metacognitive skill (reflecting on the processes of learning) is basic to problemsolving, troubleshooting, and to working one's way through difficult, unpatterned situations. Thus, assessment becomes part of the learning experience and not something that is merely tacked on and devoid of context. In the "real world," you don't take periodic paper and pencil tests to measure how well you're doing. You do your job, and that involves assessment that has to do with product quality, customer satisfaction, worker productivity, and so on.

Fourth, alternative assessment strategies and resulting accountability will force intransigent teachers to change the way they teach children. Portfolios, student recordkeeping, journals, reflective discussions, and other related alternative assessment procedures are themselves metacognitive learning experiences and are, therefore, shapers of the school day. The amount of student-to-student interaction increases, the amount of time spent in reflective thinking increases, and before teachers and students know it they have stepped off the conveyor belt that passes for learning and have entered a more seamless world where such things as planning, activity, and assessment flow together. At least that's the argument. Ellis writes, "these are not strategies that culminate in letter grades. These are strategies to be used by those teachers and students who are truly desirous of finding out what is being learned (Ellis, 1991, p. 31)."

ALTERNATIVE ASSESSMENT STRATEGIES

A number of assessment strategies for teachers (see Fig. 12.1) has emerged from all this. These strategies, or activities, are thought to be useful for measuring and enhancing critical thinking skills and the application of knowledge. With the exception of portfolios, these strategies are not particularly new; good teachers are already using them extensively in their classrooms. What is new, however, is the drive to replace the dominance of standardized tests in the eyes of the public and policymakers with these assessment techniques. At the more extreme edges of the argument, enthusiasts wish to replace grades and tests completely with these strategies.

Our review of the literature on this topic turned up only a few thoughtful pieces that seriously question the trend toward alternative assessment. A cautionary note is sounded by Worthen (1993), who has provided a careful analysis of the issues imbedded in the alternative assessment movement. We have included some of his more salient points in Figure 12.2. There are few surprises in his critique, but anyone who seriously sets out on the alternative assessment trail needs to consider these possible objections.

FIGURE 12.1. SEVEN COMMON FORMS OF PERFORMANCE ASSESSMENT

---

1. **Constructed-response items** require students to produce an answer to a question rather than to select from an array of possible answers (as in multiple-choice tests). Examples include filling in a blank, solving a mathematics problem, or writing short answers.

2. **Essays** have long been used to assess a student's understanding of a subject by having the student write a description, analysis, explanation, or summary in one or more paragraphs. Essays are used to demonstrate how well a student can use facts in context and structure a coherent discussion.

3. **Writing** is the most common subject tested by performance assessment methods. Writing enables students to demonstrate composition skills, as well as their knowledge of language, syntax, and grammar.

4. **Oral discourse** was the earliest form of performance assessment. Oral interviews can be used in assessment of young children, when written testing is inappropriate. An obvious use of oral assessment is in foreign languages.

5. **Exhibitions** are designed as comprehensive demonstrations of skills or competence. Exhibitions require a broad range of competencies, are often interdisciplinary in focus, and require student initiative and creativity.

6. **Experiments** are used to test how well a student understands scientific concepts and can carry out scientific processes. Activities to be assessed include developing hypotheses, planning and carrying out experiments, writing-up findings, using the skills of measurement and estimation, and applying knowledge of scientific facts and underlying concepts.

7. **Portfolios** are collections of a student's work assembled over time. As students create their portfolios, they must evaluate their own work, a key feature of performance assessment. Portfolios are most common in writing and language arts—showing drafts, revisions, and works in progress.

Source: Adapted from Feuer, M.J., & Fulton, K. (1993). "The Many Faces of Performance Assessment." *Phi Delta Kappan, 74,* 478.

FIGURE 12.2. CRITICAL ISSUES FACING ALTERNATIVE ASSESSMENT

Conceptual clarity. As yet, there is too little coherence to the concepts and language being used about alternative assessment, performance assessment, authentic assessment, direct assessment, and practical testing.

Mechanisms for self-criticism. Internal self-criticism is rather scarce among proponents of alternative assessment. If voices of caution are drowned out by the clamor for more rapid adoption of methods of alternative assessment, advocates could easily forget that self-criticism is the only road to continuing improvement.

Support from well-informed educators. The success or failure of the movement will depend on the willingness and competence of the teachers in the classrooms to undertake such tasks. This implies teachers with a higher degree of assessment competencies which differ from what is required now.

Technical quality and truthfulness. What technical specifications and criteria should be used to judge the quality of the assessments, including reliability and validity? The crux of the matter is whether or not the alternative assessment movement will be able to show that its assessments accurately reflect a student's true abilities which are relevant to adult life.

Standardization of assessment judgments. How to standardize criteria and performance levels sufficiently to support necessary comparisons without causing them to lose the power and richness of assessment tailored to the student's needs and achievements remains a daunting issue.

Ability to assess complex thinking skills. Do alternative modes of assessment necessarily require the use of more complex processes by students? Proponents cannot assume that students are using such skills just because they are performing a hands-on task.

Acceptability to stakeholders. The public's acceptance of alternative assessment is not a sure thing. Alternative assessments are difficult to use to report learning outcomes for entire classes, school districts, or state systems. Political realities demand such accountability.

Appropriateness for high-stakes assessment. Does alternative assessment provide sufficient standardization to defend high-stakes decisions based on such measures? Will ethnic minorities score better on alternative assessments than on traditional measures—or more poorly, as now appears quite possible? Will the inevitable legal challenges aimed at high-stake decisions based on alternative assessments be more difficult to defend because of validity and reliability questions?

Feasibility. One of the most frequently debated issues is whether or not alternative assessment is feasible for large-scale efforts to assess student performance. Does alternative assessment produce sufficiently greater benefits to justify its increased costs?

Source: Adapted from Worthen, B. (1993). Critical Issues That Will Determine the Future of Alternative Assessment. Phi Delta Kappan, 74, 444–54.

EVALUATING ALTERNATIVE ASSESSMENT

POTENTIAL AND PITFALLS

There is an underlying assumption here that teachers and students are not presently doing the types of assessment advocated by the movement. To the extent that this is true, the alternative assessment movement is vital, and it could lead to fundamental changes in education. All of us can readily agree that learning is more than doing well on standardized or written tests, and classroom evaluation needs to reflect that. For this reason alone we applaud these efforts. As Rayborn (1992, p. 24) notes, "no alternative currently available represents a magic bullet in the quest for the perfect way to assess student achievement."

Worthen's critique (1993), while not at all an attempt to hit alternative assessment below the waterline, is a useful primer on what might go wrong. The issues of conceptual clarity, standardization, public acceptance, feasibility, and technical quality, to name a few, are not trivial concerns. Standardization, for example, is seen by many as irrelevant today, a throwback to the days of industry, left over as an artifact in today's information society. But we are at least 50 years into the collecting process of standardized test scores. To throw out such a means of achievement comparison in favor of something that has little empirical evidence behind it could prove to be a dangerous move. Goodwill, enthusiasm, and a chorus of true believers will not ultimately bring about the paradigm shift called for by the leaders of the alternative assessment movement. It will take something more intellectually persuasive. The answer may prove to be that we need both.

EDUCATIONAL RESEARCH AND ALTERNATIVE ASSESSMENT

There is very little, if anything, in the literature about research on this topic other than anecdotal reports of what types of alternative assessments are being used. Researchers have yet to address the questions of whether or not the use of such assessment strategies actually changes teacher behavior, or whether this results in greater learning by students. Either of these pursuits would lend itself quite readily to empirical research. If and when researchers focus on this latter question, there will be inherent methodological problems with the research, namely that of determining satisfactory educational outcomes and methods of assessing those outcomes. Alternative assessment advocates may balk at the use of standardized tests scores as measures of achievement, resulting in no satisfactory way to compare groups. Thus, the overall effect of this movement on student learning may prove to be difficult to document. Its efficacy would then necessarily be defended on the basis of the belief that it focuses teaching and learning on more purposeful pursuits.

REFERENCES

Cronin, J.F. (1993). Four misconceptions about authentic learning. *Educational Leadership*, 50(7), 78–80.

Ellis, A.K. (1991). Evaluation as problemsolving. *Curriculum in Context*, 19(2), 30–31.

Lehman, N. (1994). Is there a science of success? *The Atlantic*

Monthly, 273(2), 83–98.

Newmann, F.M., & Wehlage, G.G. (1993). Five standards of authentic instruction. *Educational Leadership*, 50(7), 8–12.

Rayborn, R. (1992). "Alternatives for assessing student achievement: Let me count the ways." In *Assessment: How Do We Know What They Know?*, 24–27. Union, WA: Washington State Association for Supervision and Curriculum Development.

Toch, T. (1991). *In the Name of Excellence: The Struggle to Reform the Nation's Schools and Why it's Failing and What Should be Done*. New York: Oxford University Press.

Worthen, B.R. (1993). Critical issues that will determine the future of alternative assessment. *Phi Delta Kappan*, 74, 444–48.

13

EDUCATIONAL TECHNOLOGY

. . . We must keep firmly in mind the thought that technology is not the answer to the problems of education. At best, technology can help us to solve the problems of education. . . . I am convinced that our children can become intellectual giants compared to us adults—if we use technology intelligently and provide teachers with the support they need.

Ludwig Braun

Trading in an old or out-of-date automobile is a common occurrence. It may be a painful or an enjoyable experience, but it happens frequently. However, how many schools do you know that have ever considered trading in their old instructional vehicle for a new model?

Steve Adams and Gerald Bailey

The most recent panacea for education's ills is the microcomputer. But despite its power and interactive capabilities, the computer remains a tool fully exploited by relatively few.

Robert Hannafin and Wilhelmina Savenye

WHAT IS EDUCATIONAL TECHNOLOGY?

Several decades ago there was great excitement in our profession over the promises of educational technology. It would make teaching easier at the very least, and it would probably revolutionize the schools. Two technologies, especially, were touted: audio/visual instruction and instructional television. Audio/visual learning labs in schools and colleges where students could go in and dial up a tape of a great lecture or speech or whatever, were put in place. Eager learners could follow along with a notesheet to take down the great ideas and wealth of information made available to them, replaying crucial excerpts, all the while learning at their own pace. Students in history or science classes could listen to assigned tapes at their own convenience. In foreign language classes students had endless opportunities to hear the language spoken by native speakers and to speak the language, playing it back to hear how they sounded. It didn't get any better than this, even at the State Fair Kitchen of the Future. The future had at long last arrived. No more dreary lectures. No more reading of dusty textbooks. The gap had been closed between the best of high technology and school itself.

The other great technological innovation was instructional television. Predictions were made that the teacher as we knew him or her would become obsolete. One really good teacher on television could teach many students. Of course, there was live broadcast, but the tapes (kinescopes early on) could be played and replayed. Now everyone could go to Harvard, or at least Harvard could come to every classroom. The teacher's job would be to turn on the set, monitor the students while they eagerly took in every sight and sound, and to carry on follow-up discussions or assignments. In the days before satellite telemetry, airplanes flew patterns over different parts of the country, beaming down educational broadcasts to several states at a time. The possibilities for spreading good teaching far beyond the classroom walls seemed limitless.

Somehow, the promises of these technologies were not fulfilled, at least not to the extent that the promises implied. These are dim memories now, but those old enough remember the initial rush of excitement from those heady days no doubt feel a sense of *déjà vu* when they are told once more that technologies will revolutionize the schools. The fact is that such predictions were made in the late 1920s with the advent of talking motion pictures, so maybe some *real* oldtimers could tell us that the promise of technology is at least as old as Gutenberg.

So it is a fair question to ask if the technological advances of the 1990s will indeed make a real difference in how teachers teach and how students learn at school. It is also reasonable to ask whether someone 25 years from now writing a book on education innovations will include similar thoughts with computers and hypermedia as their examples of promises to keep. We'll have to wait and see.

A question asked by the proponents of educational technology is the degree to which our current methodologies and curriculum meet the needs of students who will live their adult lives in the 21st Century. It is a good question and one we should all care about. The answer given by technology advocates is no. They rightly point out that the needs of students are far greater than just knowing how to operate a computer. They call for a total restructuring of education, and they see technology as offering hope that the restructuring will be genuine.

It must be noted here that we are not concerned with

specific courses in *how* to operate a computer or write a computer program, that is, training in how to *use* technology. Those are complex, necessary technical skills, of course. What proponents of educational technology are talking about is the use of technologies to fundamentally restructure education: the business of how teachers teach and how students learn. Visionaries such as Seymour Papert, author of the books *Mindstorms* (1980) and *Children's Machine* (1993), advocate a total restructuring which would replace textbooks, frontal teaching, and passive learning environments with networks to a wealth of information increasingly available through electronic access to knowledge.

The so-called Information Highway using microcomputers, videodisks, CD-ROM, hypercards, camcorders, VCR's, multimedia facilities, telecommunications, satellite telemetry using uplinks and downlinks, online databases, modems, and virtual reality is exciting or frightening, depending on your perspective. Educational technologists challenge not merely the ways schools are run and how students learn, but whether school as we know it even ought to be the seat of learning. Gone would be the traditional reliance on seat-time, attendance as learning, whole-class instruction, teachers, and education as a school-based phenomenon. In its place would be a brave new technological world in which students would become self-directed learners, working together to solve real problems, and able to access information anywhere in the world (see Figures 13.1 and 13.2).

Adams and Bailey (1993) pose a series of questions against which educators might take the measure of the schools' potential for success in preparing students for an information age. An important consideration, they suggest, transcends the obvious availability of technology. They ask what is being proposed beyond the obligatory computer in every room and satellite dish on the roof of every school, which we would suggest is merely the high tech version of "a chicken in every pot and a car in every garage." Fundamental questions to be asked include: Are students active participants in their own learning?; Do students' educational experiences mirror daily life, reality, and the world of work?; Are students learning from technology-driven curriculum materials that provide current,

---

FIGURE 13.1. ESSENTIAL ELEMENTS OF A RESTRUCTURED
SCHOOL

◆ Technology should be integral part of restructured schools.

◆ The student must take on a new role as active learner.

◆ The teacher must assume a new role as counselor, research associate, mentor resource allocator, and advisor.

◆ School schedules must change in the direction of block scheduling to provide longer learning sessions.

◆ Team teaching and an interdisciplinary approach are essentials.

◆ Shared decisionmaking is an essential ingredient.

◆ Cooperative learning, peer teaching, and sharing of ideas should replace the standard practice of students working in isolation.

◆ The current concept of the classroom must be replaced by the concept of the world as the classroom accessible by students.

◆ Parental and community involvement in the school must be increased significantly.

◆ New assessment tools must be found to assess student learning.

Source: Adapted from Braun, L. (1993). Educational Technology: Help for All the Kinds. *The Computing Teacher* (May), p. 14.

diverse, and rich information?; Do students access information using a wide variety of emerging technologies? Do teachers use performance-based assessment to measure student achievement?; Do teachers use multiple technology-based learning models to facilitate learning?; Do teachers and students believe in an information literacy curriculum that focuses on accessing, analyzing, applying, and creating information using electronic or technology-based learning models? Such questions are more than questions about technology and its applications to school life; they challenge educators to completely reexamine their ideas of the teaching and learning process.

FIGURE 13.2. COMMON EDUCATIONAL TECHNOLOGIES

◆ Computers can be used for self-paced personalized learning activities and can be combined to make interactive networks.

◆ Compact Disk Read Only Memory (CD-ROM) has both audio and visual capabilities and may be used to store an entire set of encyclopedias or other sets of books in a very small space. Videodisks can store tremendous amounts of information on 12-inch disks and can produce a very high quality video and audio presentation. They can also be used with other technologies to create multimedia presentations.

◆ Scanners can be used to enter text and graphics into the computer very quickly for editing and desktop publishing.

◆ Television, camcorders, and audio and video recorders can be combined with a computer to produce multimedia applications.

◆ Multimedia is the integration of various technologies into interactive medium involving text, graphics video, and sound. Two of the most common authoring systems are Hypercard for Apple computers and Linkway for IBM computers.

◆ Electronic mail, modems, and FAX machines allow students to have direct contact with a variety of databases and to send and receive information.

◆ Two-way interactive networks allow students and teachers to have direct visual and auditory contact from different, and sometimes distant, locations.

Source: Adams, S., & Bailey, G. (1993) Education for the Information Age: Is it time to Trade Vehicles? *NASSP Bulletin* (May).

PROMISES TO KEEP?

The excitement that accompanies technological advances is compelling. There is, however, a dark side to all this. An interesting analysis is offered by Hannafin and Savenye (1993). They observed that "Each technological 'breakthrough' in the past resulted in disappointment followed by disillusionment and eventually abandonment (p. 26)." Why is this so? They suggest, and a number of others agree, that teachers are the culprit. Teachers have resisted the integration of technology into their classes because of the additional time and effort needed to learn and implement the technology, lack of confidence in its efficacy, poor quality software (this excuse is wearing increasingly thin), and good old-fashioned fear of machines. Beyond these more obvious factors, Hannafin and Savenye build a strong case that the problems are more philosophical than this. They note that for the first time in any serious way, "the traditional role of the teacher—that of lecturer, imparter of knowledge, and controller of activities—was being replaced (pp. 26–27)." They maintain that for technology to make a difference in the schools, "an underlying change in learning theory" must take place in education. Not only must teachers change their management and learning theories, but so must the whole of society:

> An innovation designed to allow students to control their own learning flies in the face of the reality of the vast bulk of today's education system. . . . If the accepted view in society is that knowledge is imparted from teacher to learner, then the notion that learning can occur by unsupervised exploring and by probing unstructured open-ended problems will probably be resisted by society (p. 29).

EVALUATING EDUCATIONAL TECHNOLOGY

POTENTIAL AND PITFALLS

When entertainment great Al Jolson routinely told his vaudeville audiences, "You ain't seen nothin' yet, folks," he was perfectly right. He was, in fact, more right than he knew. Technologies in the form of motion pictures, radio, and television pushed vaudeville into the dustbins of history. Gag men and funny ladies were forced to restructure their entire acts. One of the ongoing complaints directed at the new order of things was that in vaudeville, with a different audience every night, you could tell the same jokes and do the same routines for years and it didn't matter. With radio, and later with television, a joke was heard, a routine was seen, by everyone in the country at once. You'd better have an entirely new routine next week. Of course, this created whole new industries for gag writers, advertising people, stagehands, etc. Popular entertainment as we know it was completely restructured, not because of some philosophical or empirically-based theory, but because technology forced it. Now we really aren't sure how far this analogy with vaudeville can be taken, but maybe, just maybe, the schools better watch out!

Here are some of the issues at stake:

◆ We may be in the curious position of finding that children feel more comfortable with new technologies than their teachers. That was probably not true of chalk and chalkboard, paper and pencil, overhead projectors, and felt pens. A revolution in computer use is happening as children use them in their homes and in arcades. Allen Glenn, an expert in educational technologies, has said that if you can remember black and white television you will probably find computer-assisted instruction difficult. What if you can remember radio?

◆ There is presently real access to information and resources around the world. A generation ago the city library and the school library really were the central repository of knowledge as far as most of us were concerned. Just as it was true in the days of vaudeville, you had to go to these places to obtain access to knowledge. In other words, the old order was not only more orderly, it was more centralized. Now as the Information Highway is built, access to knowledge will becoming increasingly bountiful, chaotic, and decentralized. What that might mean for school-as-central-place is problematic to say the least.

Not long ago, as part of the background research for this

chapter, we sat in a television studio and watched as a teacher of Russian language taught her subject to high school students in rural schools scattered across the states of Washington, Idaho, and the province of British Columbia. She and her students were linked through satellite telemetry into an electronic classroom. As she taught with great animation, students would call in asking her questions which she fielded with the skill of a major league shortstop. These students, who came from schools too small to warrant the hiring of teachers of Russian, Japanese, and in some cases, physics and advanced mathematics, are able to take advantage of the opportunity to learn from skilled, specialized instructors who simply were unavailable to them in the recent past.

Educational technology offers great promise for changing the nature of schooling, but it will not be an easy task in spite of such scenarios as we spun in the previous paragraph. Without a change in learning theory, vast amounts of dollars may be spent on technological equipment that will sit idle or be used sparingly, amounting to little more than expensive toys for children or as rewards for students to use after they have finished their "real" school work.

Another potential problem is the disparity that may develop between schools and districts able to afford or have access to technology, or that can develop partnerships with businesses that can supply the equipment, and those districts that cannot. A related issue is the in-home access to technology that many middle and upper class children already enjoy, an access mainly denied to the poor. The rich, whether at home or school, will get richer and the poor will lag behind. This is a difficult issue indeed. One thing is clear, however, and that is the fact that denying those who can afford it will not particularly help those who cannot. It is an equity issue, and we think the only reasonable answer is to support the use of technology as much as possible in "poor" schools.

Finally, there is the recurring complaint that as students become more comfortable with technology they tend to withdraw from what Robert Reich calls the "world of real people, engaged in the untidy and difficult struggle with real problems." Technology has created a new sense of personal space. Headsets, computer screens, and video games, not to mention the coming Virtual Reality, have made it possible to "communicate" almost endlessly without other human beings. That may indeed be a problem, but traditional instruction has produced little evidence of superiority. Researcher John Goodlad has noted that in school settings students tend to learn alone in groups. The fiction of students in classrooms busily engaged in shared learning is not the best argument against the isolation of the high-tech learner. Two things are significant here. First is the great need for research in this area. To what extent does technology interfere or expedite socially-constructed knowledge and shared experience? Second, what needs to happen in order to produce learning experiences that successfully integrate technology with socialization of the young?

EDUCATIONAL TECHNOLOGY AND EDUCATIONAL RESEARCH

Level 1 research is primitive at this point. More than a decade ago Clark (1983) questioned the atheoretical nature of the field and maintained that researchers should stop exploring the relationship between media and learning until a new learning theory or paradigm was developed. He maintained that "media are mere vehicles that deliver instruction but do not influence student achievement any more than the truck that delivers our groceries causes changes in our nutrition (p. 445)." In an effort to address these concerns, Kozma (1991) attempted to provide such a theoretical framework. Kozma's theory is one of "the learner actively collaborating with the medium to construct knowledge," and he sees it standing "in vivid contrast to an image in which learning occurs as the result of instruction being 'delivered' by some (or any) medium (p. 179)." Kozma's theory is concerned with how media characteristics affect the structure, formation, and modification of mental models:

> In this theoretical framework, learning is viewed as an active, constructive process whereby the learner strategically manages the available cognitive resources to create new knowledge by extracting information from the environment and integrating it with information already stored in memory (p. 180).

Essentially, Kozma views learning with media as a complementary, interactive process in which knowledge is constructed, "sometimes by the learner and sometimes by the medium." (p. 179) Kozma, on the basis of his review of the research, concludes that Clark's (1983) contention that media do not influence learning under any circumstances is not supported by research. There is no evidence that theory has been the driving force in research efforts to advance the use of educational technology.

Much of the Level 2 and Level 3 research in educational technology is directed toward the use of computers. Designers and users of multimedia appear to be still developing its role in the learning process, so the research is emergent but certainly not definitive. The new generation of multimedia involves extensive use of the computer, so what were separate studies a few years ago (for example, audio/visual learning), are now inextricably linked. Although the computer may be a relatively new entry on the educational scene, there are a considerable number of published research studies and reviews of the research. Our own examination of the research literature in this area leads us to conclude that it is necessary to mention some issues pertaining to the research before we discuss the findings.

Research in educational technology is somewhat confounding (as it is in many areas of education) because it is very difficult to isolate the single technology variable to show cause and effect. Even when one discovers efficacious outcomes in the learning process, one is seldom sure of exactly which of several variables (for example, teacher presence, motivation, teaching/learning method), might be interacting with the technology itself. This is not an insurmountable problem, but in research terms, this means that rival hypotheses are many times uncontrolled in the studies. Also, the technologies used in studies do not form consistent treatments, that is the technology may be used in different ways by different programs or teachers. For example, determining the effectiveness of computers in the classroom is confounded by the differential usage (for example, teacher-guided vs. independent learning) of hardware and software by teachers.

All of this has to do with the quality of the research, and

several reviewers have documented these problems (*i.e.,* Becker, 1987; and Clark, 1992; 1991; 1985a; 1985b). This is not to say that we must throw up our hands and admit to knowing nothing, but we must be somewhat cautious about accepting uncritically many of the specific findings at this point. Consequently, we are willing to say only in very general terms what we think the research says. Because of the very large number of individual studies in educational technology, many published and many unpublished, we think it advisable for practitioners to begin with a look at the considerable number of recent reviews of the research in this area (Liao, 1992; Cotton, 1991; Kulik & Kulik, 1991; 1987; Kozma, 1991; McNeil & Nelson, 1991; Ryan, 1991; Roblyer, 1988; Niemiec, Weinstein, & Walberg, 1987). Given the limitations mentioned above, we are comfortable in saying that there is considerable support in the research for the use of technology, especially computers in the teaching/learning process. In general it appears that:

1. The integration of computers with traditional instruction produces higher academic achievement in a number of subject areas than does traditional instruction alone.

2. Students learn more quickly and with greater retention when learning with the aid of computers.

3. Computers seem to produce especially greater learning gains with elementary students and with low achievers.

4. Students like learning with computers, and their attitudes toward learning and school are positively affected by computer use.

5. Effective and adequate teacher training is an integral element of successful learning programs based on or assisted by technology.

Generalizations 1 through 4 could hold up rather well over time, or they may be a factor of the Hawthorne Effect which stipulates that most any novel intervention raises productivity in the short-term. Generalization 5 could probably be made about any teaching/learning protocol.

To return to our vaudeville analogy, we think that a revolution in access to knowledge is taking place all around us. And just as the old forms of entertainment no longer were sufficient, so will the old forms of school no longer be adequate. As we write this book, we are able to call up literature searches on our computer screen, something that was not possible just a few years ago. You have access to databases in forms and content that you wouldn't have believed possible in the past. So, at least for some, the information age is qualitatively different from the industrial age from which we have emerged. But two issues remain: that of equity or the provision of access to the new knowledge forms for all, rich and poor alike, and whether the quality of the experience with all the new information will improve the life of learners. We think it can. But there are those who still claim vaudeville was better than radio or television, not because it was more slick, but because it had a live, human element to it. And to return to our comments of a moment ago regarding better technology for writers, we have no evidence that technology will produce improvements over Dickens, Dostoevsky, or Austen.

REFERENCES

Adams, S., & Bailey, G. (1993). Education for the Information Age: Is It Time To Trade Vehicles? *NASSP Bulletin* (May).

Becker, H.J. (1987). *The Impact of Computer Use on Children's Learning: What Research Has Shown and What it Has Not.* Paper presented at the Annual Meeting of the American Educational Research Association, April 20–24, 1987, Washington, DC (ERIC Document Reproduction Service No. ED287458)

Braun, L. (1993). Educational Technology: Help for All the Kinds. *The Computing Teacher* (May).

Clark, R.E. (1983). Reconsidering research on learning from Media. *Review of Educational Research, 53*(4), 445–59.

Clark, R.E. (1985a). Evidence for confounding in computer-based instruction studies: Analyzing the meta-analysis. *Educational Communication and Technology, 33*(4), 249–62.

Clark, R.E. (1985b). Confounding in educational computing research. *Journal of Educational Computing Research, 1*(2), 137–48.

Clark, R.E. (1991). When researchers swim upstream: Reflections on an unpopular argument about learning from media. *Educational Technology, 31*(2), 34–40.

Clark, R.E. (1992). Dangers in the evaluation of instructional media. *Academic Medicine, 67*(12), 819–20.

Cotton, K. (1991). *Computer-Assisted Instruction*. Portland, OR: Northwest Regional Educational Laboratory.

Hannafin, R.D., & Savenye, W.C. (1993). Technology in the classroom: The teacher's new role and resistance to it. *Educational Technology* (June), 26–31.

Kozma, R.B. (1991). Learning with media. *Review of Educational Research, 61*(2), 179–211.

Kulik, J.E., & Kulik, C.L. (1987). *Computer-Based Instruction: What 200 Evaluations Say*. Ann Arbor, MI: Center for Research on Learning and Teaching, University of Michigan. (ERIC Document Reproduction Service No. ED285521).

Kulik, C.L., & Kulik, J.A. (1991). Effectiveness of computer-based instruction: An updated analysis. *Computers in Human Behavior, 7*(1–2), 75–94.

Liao, Y.K. (1992). Effects of computer-assisted instruction on cognitive outcomes: A meta-analysis. *Journal of Research on Computing in Education, 24*, 367–80.

McNeil, B.J., & Nelson, K.R. (1991). Meta-analysis of interactive video instruction: A 10-year review of achievement effects. *Journal of Computer-Based Instruction, 18*, 1–6.

Niemiec, R., Weinstein, T., & Walberg, H.J. (1987). The effects of computer-based instruction in elementary schools: A quantitative synthesis. *Journal of Research on Computing in Education, 20*, 85–103.

Papert, S. (1980). *Mindstorms: Children, Computers and Powerful Ideas*. New York: Basic Books.

Papert, S. (1993). *Children's Machines*. New York: Basic Books.

Roblyer, M.D. (1988). The effectiveness of microcomputers in education: A review of the research from 1980–1987. *Technological Horizons in Education Journal, 16*(2), 85–89.

Ryan, A.W. (1991). Meta-analysis of achievement effects of microcomputer applications in elementary schools. *Educational Administration Quarterly, 27(2),* 161–84.

14

COOPERATIVE LEARNING[1]

An essential instructional skill that all teachers need is knowing how and when to structure students' learning goals competitively, individualistically and cooperatively. Each goal structure has its place; an effective teacher will use all three appropriately.

David and Roger Johnson

The future of cooperative learning is difficult to predict. My hope is that even when cooperative learning is no longer the "hot new method," schools and teachers will continue to use it as a routine part of instruction. My fear is that cooperative learning will largely disappear as a result of the faddism so common in American Education.

Robert Slavin

Oh, they had cooperative learning when I was a kid; they just didn't call it that. They called it cheating.

former teacher Arlen King

---

[1] Portions of this chapter appear in our earlier book *Research on Educational Innovations* (1993), and are used with permission of the publisher, Eye on Education, Princeton, NJ.

WHAT IS COOPERATIVE LEARNING?

Cooperative learning may well be the biggest educational innovation of our time. It has permeated every level of teacher training from preservice to inservice. It is estimated that more that 30,000 teachers and would-be teachers have been trained at the Minneapolis-based Cooperative Learning Center alone. And cooperative learning is not a peculiarly American educational phenomenon. It is touted from Israel to New Zealand, from Sweden to Japan.

We address the cooperative learning phenomenon in this book on restructuring because we feel it meets a condition that other, basically classroom-oriented, programs do not meet, or at least have not empirically demonstrated they meet. The condition we refer to is a transformative condition. Let us show you what we mean. The research of John Goodlad (1984), Philip Jackson (1968), and others has shown empirically that students in traditional classrooms have very little opportunity to engage in student-to-student interaction. Most sanctioned classroom talk is teacher-to-student interaction. Such an impoverished level of student-initiated talk (Goodlad, 1984, estimates 7 minutes per day), inhibits intellectual, linguistic, and moral growth (Vygotsky, 1986; Piaget, 1970). The spontaneous learning that Piaget said was essential, the socially-constructed knowledge that Vygotsky described, and the business of "finding one's own voice" that Habermas (1974) said is basic to democracy itself, will emerge only when students talk to each other in productive ways. The difference between a classroom set in rows with every student working alone and one where students actually work and talk together is a transformational difference.

The research claims that detail the elements of cooperative learning are more elaborate and documented than those of any other movement in education today. Study after study finds its way into the scholarly journals. Literally hundreds of articles, from research to practice, appear annually on this topic. All the major professional subject matter associations have published special editions showing how cooperative learning can be used in mathematics, social studies, language arts, science, etc.

The claims made on behalf of cooperative learning are legendary. Seemingly, it can solve any educational problem. Researcher Robert Slavin (1989/90), himself a recognized authority in the field of cooperative learning warns:

> Another danger inherent in the success of cooperative learning is that the methods will be oversold and undertrained. It is being promoted as an alternative to tracking and within class grouping, as a means of mainstreaming academically handicapped students, as a means of improving race relations in desegregated schools, as a solution to the problems of students at risk, as a means of increasing prosocial behavior among children, as well as a method for simply increasing the achievement of all students. Cooperative learning can in fact accomplish this staggering array of objectives, but not as a result of a single three-hour inservice session (p. 3).

Of course, Slavin is perfectly correct that a brief introduction to such a complex idea is hardly sufficient to accomplish anything more than a sense of what cooperative learning is. But note his agreement with the wide range of educational problems that cooperative learning can productively address! If it could do half these things, it would be the pedagogical equivalent of a cure for cancer.

What is this apparently wonderful thing called cooperative

learning? How does it work? Can it really bring about fundamental changes for the better in classroom life? Let's take a closer look at it so that you can begin to decide for yourself.

COOPERATIVE LEARNING MODELS

Cooperative learning takes on many different forms in classrooms, but they all involve students working in groups or teams to achieve certain educational goals. Beyond the most basic premise of working together, students must also depend on each other, a concept called positive interdependence. From here cooperative learning takes on specific traits advocated differentially by different developers. In some cases, cooperative learning is conceived of as a generic strategy that one could use in practically any setting or in any course of study. In other cases, cooperative learning is conceived of as a subject-matter specific strategy.

The idea of the group is at the heart of cooperative learning. As Johnson and Johnson (1994) point out, not every group is effective. All of us have been part of groups that essentially wasted time, were inefficient, and that produced a product that was of low quality. And all of us have heard students say at one time or another, "That's the last time I'll work with them; I did all the work, and they shared in the credit." The Johnsons have done some very useful thinking and writing in this area, producing ideas about what is and what is not a cooperative group.

Five or more major models of cooperative learning exist. They have much in common, but the differences among them provide useful distinctions. All five represent training programs for teachers who, having taken the training, should be equipped to implement the various attendant strategies in their classrooms.

David and Roger Johnson of the University of Minnesota are the authors of the Learning Together model. The model is based in a generic group process theory applicable to all disciplines and grade levels. Students are placed in formal or informal base groups which are charged with solving problems, discussing issues, carrying out projects, etc.

The Johnson and Johnson model is built on five elements

which trace back to the theories of Morton Deutsch (1949). The first element is positive interdependence in which students must believe that they are linked with other students to the point that they cannot succeed unless the other students also succeed. The second element is that of face-to-face interaction in which students must converse with each other, helping one another with the learning tasks, problems, and novel ideas. The third element is individual accountability in which each student must be held accountable for his or her performance with the results given to both the individual and the group. The fourth element is social skills in which students are taught, and must use, appropriate group interaction skills as part of the learning process. The fifth element is group processing of goal achievement in which student groups must regularly monitor what they are accomplishing and how the group and individuals might function more effectively. Obviously teachers must be trained in these elements, and they must be able to teach them to their students in turn.

Robert Slavin of Johns Hopkins University has developed a cooperative learning model called Student Team Learning. His model is less generic than that of the Johnsons. In fact, it has at least four permutations, each of which is specifically designed to address different concerns. For example, his Cooperative Integrated Reading and Composition (CIRC) model is specifically designed for learning reading and writing in grades 3 through 6. His Team Assisted Individualization (TAI) model is designed for mathematics learning in grades 3 through 6. Slavin's approach to cooperative learning represents a sophisticated set of strategies which, as he has stated, cannot be acquired in a 3 hour workshop session.

Other notable models include that of Shlomo and Yael Sharan of Israel, which is a general plan for organizing a classroom using a variety of cooperative tactics for different disciplines; that of Spencer Kagan, whose Structural Approach includes such intriguing procedures as Roundrobin, Corners, Numbered Head Together, Roundtable, and Match Mine; and Elliot Aronson's Jigsaw, composed of interdependent learning teams for academic content applicable to various age groups. Figure 14.1 illustrates the several models which we have described in these paragraphs.

FIGURE 14.1. COOPERATIVE LEARNING ADVOCATES AND THEIR MODELS

Researcher/Educator	Model	Focus
David Johnson & Roger Johnson	**Learning Together** • Formal, Informal, and Cooperative Base Groups	Generic group process theory and skills for the teacher for developing a cooperative classroom. Applicable to all levels and disciplines.
Robert Slavin	**Student Team Learning** • Student Teams-Achievement Divisions (STAD) • Teams-Games-Tournament (TGT) • Team Assisted Individualization (TAI) • Cooperative Integrated Reading and Composition (CIRC)	STAD & TGT—general techniques adaptable to most disciplines and grade levels. TAI—specifically for grades 3-6 mathematics. CIRC—specifically for grades 3-6 reading and writing.
Shlomo Sharan & Yael Sharan	**Group Investigation**	A general plan for organizing a classroom using a variety of cooperative strategies for several disciplines.
Spencer Kagan	**Structural Approach** • Roundrobin • Corners • Numbered Heads Together • Roundtable • Match Mine	"Content-free" ways of organizing social interaction in the classroom and for a variety of grade levels.
Elliot Aronson	**Jigsaw**	Interdependent learning teams for academic material which can be broken down into sections; for varying age groups.

Used properly, cooperative learning is designed to supplement and complement direct instruction and the other teaching/learning activities typical of classroom life. Its main function is to replace much of the individual, often competitive seatwork that so dominates American classrooms. From the amount of talking time made possible to each student to the actual rearrangement of chairs, desks, and tables, classrooms that make the change to cooperative learning are truly restructured.

It should be noted, as well, that advocates of cooperative learning are not necessarily opposed to individualistic and competitive learning. Their opposition is to its near complete dominance. Most cooperative learning advocates will say that there is a time and place for each type of learning, but that there must be considerably more cooperative learning in classrooms than is presently the case.

Slavin's perspective is typical of the movement when he states that "cooperative learning methods share the idea that students work together to learn and are responsible for one another's learning as well as their own" (Slavin, 1991, p. 73). Slavin's well-stated phrase sums up the essence of cooperative learning. Read it carefully.

EVALUATING COOPERATIVE LEARNING

POTENTIAL AND PITFALLS

Cooperative learning has the potential to be an important contributor to the restructuring of education. When implemented properly, it requires students to learn in a manner in which most are not accustomed. Research has shown that it can lead to greater achievement, but just as important is the potential of cooperative learning to increase problemsolving skills, and to help students work *with* other students, rather than *competing* with them. Of course, this is dependent on the acceptance of those educational outcomes as important and vital for this generation of learners. When cooperative learning is selected for this reason, it can play an important part in an authentic, participatory, fundamental (Quadrant I; see Chapter 3, Fig. 3.4) restructuring effort.

While we believe that cooperative learning can be an important part of restructuring efforts, it seems to us that it, alone, will not lead to fundamental changes of large magnitudes. When it is attempted within the same bureaucratic atmosphere of the current school setting, its impact can be greatly diminished. For example, when cooperative learning is used with the existing curriculum and evaluation procedures, it will change some aspects of the educational experience. But when it is used with an integrated curriculum and coupled with alternative assessment procedures, the changes in the learning experience will be even more fundamental. The same would be true when cooperative learning is coupled with multiage grouping, whole language learning philosophy, schools-within-schools, or an efficacious use of educational technology.

Cooperative learning does have potential pitfalls for the reformers. First, there is cooperative learning and then there is cooperative learning. As Slavin stated earlier in this chapter regarding its implementation, it will not happen "as a result of a single three-hour inservice session" for teachers. There are certain factors that must be present in the cooperative learning approach, and it is not as easy to implement cooperative learning strategies as some might think. This means that the potential exists for the "we tried that" syndrome a year or two later. It is also possible that some people expect too much from cooperative learning alone. It is not a cure for all the schools' ills, but it can be an important element of fundamental restructuring. Finally, when mandated by the administration or others from outside, it will most probably result in an arbitrary restructuring effort, with inappropriate implementation in the classrooms.

THE RESEARCH BASE FOR COOPERATIVE LEARNING

The Level 1 research can be traced back to the theories of group dynamics and social interaction developed in the 1930s and 1940s by pioneer researcher Kurt Lewin. As Slavin (1986, p. 276) notes, "A long tradition of research in social psychology has established that group discussion, particularly when group members must publicly commit themselves, is far more effective at changing individuals' attitudes and behaviors than even the most persuasive lecture."

Lewin's ideas were further refined by the social psychologist Morton Deutsch, who derived a theory of group process based on shared goals and rewards. Deutsch (1949) postulated, on the basis of his studies, that when a group is rewarded on the basis of the behavior of its members, the group members will encourage one another to do whatever helps the group to be rewarded.

The work of Lewin, Deutsch, and others led to new perceptions about the power of truly integrated groups to get things done, to sanction and support members, and to provide a whole that is greater than the sum of its parts. It is, of course, in one form or another, an old idea, and to their credit, cooperative learning advocates admit this rather freely. Socrates, for example, used cooperative dialogue between teacher and pupil in order to advance learning. What may have been felt or even known intuitively by some over the centuries (King Arthur's legendary Round Table comes to mind), now had a basis of empirical support. This set the stage for researchers to focus on the efficacy of cooperative group learning in school settings.

At Level 2, the sheer amount of empirical evidence which has accumulated from research studies in cooperative learning is staggering. There are literally of hundreds of published individual studies, as well as numerous reviews, syntheses, and meta-analyses. There appears to be no review, synthesis, or meta-analysis that concludes that cooperative learning is deficient as a means to raise student achievement. In general, all the conclusions are the same, and all are supportive.

Slavin's (1991) synthesis of the research on cooperative learningyields four main conclusions, each of which is consistent with the pure or basic research and theoretical model derived from Lewin, Deutsch, and others. The conclusions are rather sweeping, but they certainly have a sound empirical foundation:

- ◆ For enhancing student achievement, the most successful approaches have incorporated two key elements: group goals and individual accountability; that is, groups are rewarded based on the individual learning of all group members.

♦ When group goals and individual accountability are clear, achievement effects of cooperative learning are consistently positive; 37 of 44 experimental/control comparisons of at least 4 weeks' duration yielded significant positive effects, and none favored traditional methods.

♦ Positive achievement effects of cooperative learning have been found to about the same degree at all grade levels from 2–12, in all major subjects of the curriculum, and in urban, rural, and suburban schools. Effects are equally positive for high, average, and low achievers.

♦ Positive effects of cooperative learning have been documented consistently for such diverse outcomes as self-esteem, intergroup relations, acceptance of academically handicapped students, attitudes toward school, and ability to work with others.

At Level 3, we find no mention of program evaluation studies that have been done for the large-scale implementation of cooperative learning. The movement has been around long enough that long-term effects at the district level should be available. Perhaps that will become a research focus in time.

Of all the educational trends we have reviewed for this book cooperative learning has the best, largest empirical base. It is not a perfect base, and as Slavin has pointed out (Slavin, 1989/90), more research is needed at senior high school levels as well as at college and university levels. He also notes that the appropriateness of cooperative learning strategies for the advancement of higher-order conceptual learning is yet to be established firmly.

But we conclude by saying that for the administrator or teacher who wishes to bring about positive change in a more or less traditional school environment, cooperative learning would seem to be well worth exploring. To do it well takes considerable training and motivation. And to convince parents and other community members that it is more than kids sharing answers with each other will take some doing. These are comments one could make about any innovation, but in this case the innovator will have little trouble finding backup evidence.

A RESEARCH AGENDA FOR COOPERATIVE LEARNING

At this point it seems that the Level 1 and Level 2 research bases are more than adequate to justify the use of cooperative learning strategies in most settings. Fittingly, new research appears right along in the educational and psychological literature. This research base can be refined to clarify the amount of cooperative learning that is optimal during the school day, with which subjects it is most efficacious, and with which age groups it is most effective. These are the tasks for university researchers.

At Level 3, there is still research to be done. Most of the Level 2 research are experimental studies of a relatively few classrooms. The question that still remains is: "Can a cooperative learning program be implemented on a large scale basis over time?" That is, can entire districts successful retrain the teaching staff to implement and sustain cooperative learning effectively? This type of question focuses not only on the value of cooperative learning, but also on the quality and effect of the staff inservice programs, as well as the degree of ownership that participants feel.

Level 2 research has shown us that cooperative learning works. Level 3 research will tell us if we can provide quality training *and* if we can convince teachers to use it as it is intended to be used.

REFERENCES

Aronson, E., Blaney, N., Stephan, C., Sikes, J., & Snapp, M. (1978). *The Jigsaw Classroom*. Beverly Hills, CA: Sage.
Deutsch, M. (1949). A theory of cooperation and competition. *Human Relations, 2,* 129–52.

Goodlad, J. (1984). *A Place Called School: Prospects for the Future.* New York: McGraw-Hill.

Habermas, J. (1974). *Theory and Practice.* London: Heinemann.

Jackson, P. (1968). *Life in Classrooms.* New York: Holt, Rinehart, and Winston.

Johnson, D., & Johnson, R. (1989). *Cooperation and Competition: Theory and Research.* Edina, MN: Interaction Book Company.

Johnson, D., & Johnson, R. (1994). *Leading the Cooperative School, 2nd ed.* Edina, MN: Interaction Book Company.

Lewin, K. (1947). *Field Theory in Social Sciences.* New York: Harper & Row.

Piaget, J. (1970). *Science of Education and the Psychology of the Child.* New York: Viking Press.

Slavin, R. (1991). Synthesis of research on cooperative learning. *Educational Leadership, 48*(5), 71–82.

Slavin, R. (1989/90). Research on cooperative learning: Consensus and controversy. *Educational Leadership, 47*(4), 52–54.

Slavin, R. (1989/90). Here to stay—or gone tomorrow. *Educational Leadership, 47*(4), 3.

Slavin, R. (1986). *Educational Psychology: Theory into Practice.* Englewood Cliffs, NJ: Prentice-Hall.

Vygotsky, L. (1986). *Thought and Language.* Cambridge, MA: MIT Press.

15

THE SEARCH FOR MEANINGFUL CHANGE

If the principal openly says this is a good idea, with steady,
strong support, then things grow.

Roger Johnson

Within most contemporary schools, the most fundamental
belief system appears to be a commitment to bureaucracy as
the only plausible, viable form of social organization.

Anne Raywid

We are more ready to try the untried when what we do is
inconsequential.

Eric Hoffer

Theodore Sizer, Chairman of the Coalition of Essential schools, has noted that "serious efforts to redesign schools must unavoidably involve all aspects of the institutions." (1986, p. 40). He says this because any move we make in such a complex system as a school will affect everything else. "Change the schedule, and the curriculum is affected" (p. 40). Of course, this is the basis of systems theory. In his books, *The Culture of the School* (1982) and *The Predictable Failure of Educational Reform* (1990), Seymour Sarason points out that schools are synergistic places where one action creates multiple interactions. While this may seem obvious, its point apparently is lost on those who fail to realize that piecemeal efforts are doomed to fail. This is why restructuring efforts must take into account schools as socially-constructed, whole entities.

If one were to ask the typical teacher or administrator the question, "Do our schools need restructuring?," the typical answer would be a resounding "Yes." There is an abiding consensus on the need to restructure our schools. Where the equation begins to break down is over the essence of the new structure. Whatever it is that we want in place of what we have reflects a set of assumptions about what is good, what is right, and what is purposeful. The educational philosopher, G. Max Wingo (1965), wrote:

> Behind every approach to teaching method, behind
> every plan for administrative organization of the
> schools, behind the structure of every school curriculum
> stands a body of accepted doctrine in the form of
> assumptions, concepts, generalizations, and values. Thus
> we structure and restructure on the basis of some
> ideology (p. 6).

Unfortunately, as Wingo points out, only rarely is ideology
subjected to careful critical analysis, and "on the occasions
when such analysis is made there are certain to be outcries
from various segments of society (p. 6)," because most of us
simply do not wish to see our cherished ideas placed under the
lens of reflective thought. We'd rather just go ahead with what
we "know" is right!

In this book we have shown you the research base, such as
it is, for a number of innovations designed to lead the way in
the school restructuring movement. These innovations represent
a wide range of programs and organizational patterns. They
run the gamut from those soundly embedded in theory and
practice to the atheoretical and faddish. Some of them are
rather attractive, and mainly what they need is the opportunity
to show educators how much they can bring to schools. But
even a theoretically and practically sound innovation cannot be
merely pasted on. For it to succeed, innovators must consider
the entire culture of school life.

Other innovations are in our opinion insufficiently sound to
bring about any lasting, meaningful change. They will make an
initial splash, bubbling up from that seemingly bottomless
wellspring of gimmicks ladled out to the unwary and the true-
believers by enthusiastic hucksters, bringing to mind H.L.
Mencken's quip that no one ever went broke underestimating
the intelligence of the American people. A floodtide of avant-
garde teachers and administrators will use the identifying
initials or acronyms for awhile, there will be a phalanx of
highly energized "developers" who will lead the way into
workshops, faculty meetings, inservice training, accompanied
by scattered implementation, some money will change hands,
and then comes the all too familiar disappearance without a
trace. And the waters are temporarily calm, at least until the

next splash.

Most restructuring efforts involve attempts to combine two or more of the innovations, in some cases quite a few of them. Some of the innovations are actually aimed in opposing directions, built on a different kind of scaffolding; that, however, doesn't seem to stop the naive but enthusiastic from pasting them together anyway. On the other hand, it seems eminently reasonable to combine such innovations as educational technology with cooperative learning, nongraded organization with team teaching and alternative assessment, or total quality management with site-based management, just to name a few possibilities. It is, in fact, the case that true restructuring would have to address a number issues.

A WALK DOWN THE BOULEVARD OF BROKEN DREAMS

We are convinced that many of our schools are truly in need of restructuring. Some may be beyond that. And we are equally convinced that most of the steps undertaken in the name of restructuring will have little long-term positive effect. This observation is borne out by the historical record. The record will show that restructuring has been going on in earnest for nearly four decades. More than that, we hope that by looking briefly at the history of the often contradictory attempts to reform schools over the past few decades, we will successfully illustrate the idea that piecemeal, jerry-rigged efforts seldom bring lasting satisfaction or success.

We can trace the American school restructuring movement back to a day in October 1957 when the USSR (now itself restructured and under new management) launched an artificial satellite, *Sputnik,* into Earth orbit, although it is true that prior notice had been delivered in such books as Rudolph Flesch's *Why Johnny Can't Read* (1955) and Arthur Bestor's *Educational Wastelands* (1953).

The launching of *Sputnik* sent shock waves across the landscape. The little grapefruit-sized sphere catapulted into earth orbit by a Soviet rocket made its rounds every 90 minutes, beeping back signals that when translated into English seemed to say, "American schools are no good, and Russian schools are outstanding." Suddenly there was interest in improving our whole system of education. The reason it needed to be improved was because it was the culprit. Congress opened the Federal purse on an unprecedented scale, granting the money necessary to support the development of a new generation of programs. The programs, which included New Math, New Science, etc., were mainly devoted to curriculum and instruction. They were not aimed at a fundamental reconstruction of schools. They did, however, call for new curricula, new methods of teaching, and related teacher training. This had the potential to be one of the great lessons in school history: that replacing one or two parts of a complex system without reconsidering the system itself is not productive, and in some cases it is actually counterproductive.

In 1958, Congress passed the National Defense Education Act (NDEA) which was designed to provide loans and scholarships for would-be teachers and for postgraduate training for inservice teachers. Large amounts of money went into the recruiting and support of teacher training for science and mathematics in particular. The very name of the NDEA makes it clear that this was a response to a perceived threat of Soviet superiority. There was, in fact, yet another reason for such widespread teacher recruitment, and that was the rapid expansion of the school-age population. Coupled together these two phenomena brought about a heretofore unequaled burst of energy and attention to the nation's schools.

It was also at this time that some researchers, notably Robert Anderson and John Goodlad (1959), proposed such reconfigurations of school life as team teaching and the nongraded school, two ideas that remain refreshingly innovative to this day. These concerns were primarily organizational, especially at the classroom level. They were getting us closer to the idea of actually restructuring schools than had the curriculum and instruction innovations. In fact, the nongraded approach is currently touted as one of the major players in the restructuring movement of the 1990s. And team teaching seems to have found a small but dedicated following in American schools.

One other historical development is worth noting. In the 1950s, James B. Conant, president of Harvard University, was commissioned by the Carnegie Corporation to conduct a study of American schools. The study, published as a book called *The American High School Today* (1959), recommended the consolidation of small schools into larger comprehensive high schools that could offer a greater range of subjects, especially courses in advanced science and mathematics. The belief that the USSR offered its students superior courses in science and mathematics made Conant's arguments seem all the more convincing. In retrospect, there are genuinely mixed feelings about the outcome of this. It may be true that a larger school will often have a better science laboratory and *maybe* even better teachers of physics and calculus, but we know that larger schools are breeding grounds of alienation. In fairness to Conant, he said that a high school with a senior class of 100 was large enough to ensure quality. But apparently what we heard is the idea that bigger is better. The school-within-a-school movement is an attempt to capture the plus side of small while reaping the benefits of a larger structure.

By 1960 the discontent with the status quo was all too evident. The call for new content, methods, teacher training and recruitment, organizational patterns, and larger schools signaled the beginning of a long trail of reform efforts which led in time to busing, entitlements, human relations training, multicultural education, effective schools, mastery learning, and the list goes on. It seems that from that time forth the pressure has been on the schools to improve, to deliver a better product, to somehow get us out of the backwaters of mediocrity and into the bright clear waters of achievement. But it hasn't happened. And here we are in the midst of today's school restructuring movement.

The latter part of the 1960s decade and much of the 1970s were given over to equity considerations, particularly tied to race and gender. The United States Supreme Court ruled in 1954, in the case of *Brown vs. the Board of Education,* that so-called separate but equal schools were in fact anything but that. The movement to desegregate the public schools was put in motion by that decision, but it took several years and a considerable amount of civil rights legislation in the mid-1960s for things to change. What flowed from these judicial and legislative acts were public policies that would restructure the schools. Thus crosscurrents of academic reform and social policy reform washed over the schools. The busing movement grew like topsy, and entitlement programs were the order of the day. Any in-depth discussion of these issues is outside the scope of this book, but let us share just one example of how these crosscurrents affected school life. John Goodlad has noted that in his study of schooling completed in the early 1980s, all the schools that were in the high achieving quartile were schools where the parents knew the school and were involved in the life of the school. How can parents and teachers be expected to carry on meaningful dialogue when students who attend the school come from all over the city because they are bussed in? Thus, we were attempting to reform the curriculum and use the schools as tools of social policy at the same time, and the result was confusion. But the point is that we were trying to reform, or, more honestly, tinker, with the existing system. The philosopher of science Thomas Kuhn notes in his book *The Structure of Scientific Revolutions* (1970), that any long-accepted paradigm begins to crumble when it simply fails to cohere as a means for solving problems, when it is unable to explain too many phenomena, and when too many situations remain anomalous.

By the 1980s we had found a new competitor as the Russian military threat obviously began to subside. This time the competition was economic, and the competitors were found in East Asia, especially Japan. The effective schools movement gained momentum, and suddenly we were focusing on time-on-task and other basics thought to lead to higher math and reading achievement. The curious thing about the entire research base that built up around this movement was that it was almost completely lacking in cause and effect studies, relying heavily instead on causal-comparative and correlational research. The main problem with such research is that its very absence of control of its object(s) of study renders it vulnerable to multiple rival hypotheses. In other words, one can never be sure of what causes what under what circumstances to happen. One is left with a great deal of guesswork at the conclusion.

NECESSARY STEPS

It is not difficult to develop a laundry list of problems with today's schools. Anyone who has been in the business for even a short time could fill a chalkboard or a computer screen with problems. We don't intend to do that here. Instead we propose a short list of issues and answers because we think some problems are more fundamental while others can be set at the margins. Thus what to take on becomes truly a matter of priority. We suggest you consider the following high priority issues along the way to restructuring environments for learning.

TOWARD A HUMAN SCALE

The social and architectural critic Lewis Mumford once noted that if one were to consider the scale at which Pompeii, the ancient and rather ordinary Roman town buried by ash and lava from Mt. Vesuvius, was built, one would soon realize that a Pompeiian citizen could walk home from the theater in less time than it takes a modern American to get his or her car out of the parking lot of a shopping mall or football stadium. Pompeii was built on a human scale.

We are convinced that the best school environments are built on a human scale. They have about them an easy access and an air of informality that allows active participation by *all* those who are directly affected by what happens there. They are generally small and almost never large. As John Goodlad (1984, p. 309) has noted, "What are the defensible reasons for operating an elementary school of more than a dozen teachers and 300 boys and girls. I can think of none." And, "Indeed, I would not want to face the challenge of justifying a senior, let alone junior, high of more than 500 to 600 students. . . " (p. 310). Where existing schools are too large, an obvious answer is schools-within-schools. Where new buildings are being proposed, build them to a human scale.

The intimacy of a smaller structure doesn't work magic, but it does allow magic to work. It allows access, making it more possible for people to know each other and to be needed, and these are not trifling matters. As a young child happily once told us when we entered an elementary school that had an enrollment of about 80 students, "I know everybody's name, and everybody knows me." Smaller structures are not inherently more moral, caring, or connected than larger structures, but they have greater potential to realize that much used and abused idea of community. If one accepts the axiom that communication, participation, and understanding are significant in the processes of learning, then one must also consider the corollary that communication, participation, and understanding are more readily accomplished with smaller numbers and smaller structures.

TOWARD CONTEXT AND CONNECTIONS

For years, the best teachers have understood what psychologists are telling us today: that human beings are "wired" to do projects. It comes naturally to us, and we employ this approach readily in such matters as reading a book, taking a vacation, or cleaning out the garage. Projects bring to teaching and learning two psychological dimensions that are often lacking in school life: (1) they are generally practical in the sense that the participants are trying to get something done that needs to be done at a particular time for a particular reason, for example, a theater production; and (2) they cut across the artificial boundaries of academic subjects, using knowledge as a tool for problem solving rather than thinking of it as an end in itself. There are those who would quarrel with this premise, but we offer it in the spirit of our American attempt to educate *all* children and not just an elite few.

We offer two glimpses of projects. One of them is the interdisciplinary project usually done by groups of students and teachers but doable in some cases by individuals, and the other is the ancient idea of the apprenticeship, common in Medieval and Colonial times as a means to entering the various guilds, crafts, or trades. Both offer students the opportunity to experience those transcendent moments so important to a fulfilled coming of age.

One school we evaluated was a senior high school that had elected to become four schools-within-the-school, with groups of teachers and students working together in teams. The teams were comprised of students of various scholastic abilities and teachers who had previously each been committed to expertise in a single subject area. During the first year of the experiment, a team that called itself the Health Sciences School was formed. The idea was that each year another team would be phased in until the four schools-within-the-school were in place. Parents and students were involved from the beginning because the school was one of choice.

The Health Sciences School was taught by a faculty that had committed itself to an interdisciplinary approach. One of the more difficult tasks they faced was that of deciding what experiences truly ought to be interdisciplinary and which experiences were better taught and learned within the confines of a specific academic discipline. The important thing that happened as such discussions went forward was that the faculty members themselves became integrated, a key first step. They decided, in turn, that a first teaching/learning priority was for the students to become integrated. The important principle they had learned was that the integration of subjects must follow the integration of people.

The Health Sciences School was able to find a good number of apprentice-type internships for students, thanks in large part to the hard work of the principal and assistant principal who spent much of their summer visiting businesses, hospitals, clinics, high tech companies, insurance firms, etc. The apprenticeships were valuable because they got the students out into the world of work and careers and because they forged a link between the academic world of the school and the "real" world of the community.

An elementary school we worked with created an interdisciplinary curriculum for intermediate-level students. In one of the interdisciplinary units, students became involved in creating a green belt on the school grounds. The project was of sufficient scope that large numbers of students were needed to form the various committees charged with specific responsibilities. The project exemplified the best of the citizenship/democracy goals we cherish for young learners.

Parents and community people became involved in the project, contributing time, materials, and even money to make it go forward. The amount of mathematics, architecture, English, geography, history, music, art, science, and other subjects the students learned was impressive. But so were the cooperative skills, the planning, the give and take, the decisionmaking, the speechmaking, and the opportunities to feel useful in the community. These students know from experience that obligation, duty, and effort are as much a part of citizenship as are liberty, freedom, and choice.

We offer these examples merely as sketches of possibilities in restructuring. We have no illusions that they are the most dramatic things you have ever read about in the annals of educational innovation. In fact, either one is something that could have been done years ago, in the days before TQM, OBE, and the other innovations you have read about in this book. Neither took a large government grant to accomplish. Neither presented itself as an experiment that would change education as we know it. These projects were efforts that valued people first and that were dedicated to helping young people experience affiliation, involvement, and camaraderie. We are convinced that people remember these kinds of educational activities far beyond the school horizon because they are experiences that make possible the transcendent moments so desperately needed by young people as they search for meaning in their lives.

We would be remiss if we did not return to a phenomenon that will restructure education, if not the schools, whether we want it to or not. That phenomenon is technology in the form of the Information Highway. The entire concept of access to knowledge is shifting as you read this. We are in the midst of a revolution that is rapidly moving knowledge from a few centralized, standardized locations to many decentralized, chaotic locales. Supermarkets carry more magazines than small town libraries did just a few years ago. A home computer of modest capability can immediately access information that you would have had to send away for in the past.

Schools, by definition and location, have represented a central place in all of modern times. A more ancient definition of school, still used in philosophy and some academic areas, is that a school is a set of related, coherent ideas about something, a kind of world view. Such a school is bound together not by geographic constraint but by the power of ideas and/or values. As technology forces knowledge to fly away from the center distributing it all over the place, we may find ourselves returning to this older sense of school.

In Chapter 4, we developed a model of educational research based on three different but related levels of the conduct of inquiry: Level 1 is basic or pure research, the purpose of which is to explore or develop theories and constructs; Level 2 is applied research, the purpose of which is to test empirically in school settings the efficacy of theoretically established ideas; and Level 3 is program evaluation research, the purpose of which is to establish what happens when an empirically-validated idea (*e.g.,* cooperative learning, mastery learning) is adopted and implemented on a broad scale such as an entire state or district. Each of the three levels is crucial to the advancement of education.

Throughout this book, we have talked about the fact that the profession has not conducted serious, well-crafted Level 3 or program evaluation research. Schools are infinitely complex ecosystems filled with a myriad of interacting variables. No matter how well-established the Level 1 and Level 2 foundations of an innovation may be, we still do not know how effectively that innovation travels at the level of widespread implementation until we have collected serious data on its everyday usage in everyday classroom situations.

Much of this serious breakdown owes to the fact that university researchers and school people have little confidence in each other. Until school people and researchers recognize that they must collaborate in the conduct of program evaluation studies (Level 3) we will be left without answers regarding the true worth of particular innovations. University scholars and school people have between them the wherewithal to do this important research. It will not be easy, and it will call upon the judicious use of quantitative and qualitative methods. No doubt new methodologies, reporting procedures, journals, etc., will emerge as a result. This is as it should be.

The school district personnel who thought that innovation meant adopting the "latest trend" will have to revise their thinking. Innovation will come to mean testing new ideas in the crucible of school life, and not merely hopping on the next bandwagon. University researchers will have to realize that program evaluation studies, however messy, are indeed worthwhile for them and their graduate students to pursue. When this coming together happens there will be the promise of true reform.

CONCLUSIONS

The current and recent history of school restructuring attempts in America is dominated by means/ends scenarios. Most of them are in fact management protocols that have shallow moral and intellectual potential primarily because they view students and teachers as objects rather than as subjects in teaching and learning, and because they hold out the promise that if we try *this* (a particular program) we're sure to get *that* (*greater* achievement).

We seem also to have become vulnerable to packaged systems that are purveyed by impresarios who have all the trends, research, and procedures you need to know right in their hip pocket. Staff development has become commercialized and institutionalized in a way that we might not have even imagined just a generation ago. Professional organizations and freelance trainers offer no end of 1-, 2-, or 3-day conferences where prepackaged solutions to unique, local problems are shamelessly doled out by people who don't even know those in attendance. Colleges and universities become accomplices, not hesitating to offer transcripted grades to those with the money to buy some credits.

It doesn't have to be this way. The best school restructuring will happen when you, your colleagues, students, parents, and interested others begin to talk and listen to each other about your dreams for young people. This is not to say that you're on your own and undeserving of outside help. There are times when outside consultants can see things you can't see clearly from within. There are times when you need to hear the ideas of others who might have some wisdom and knowledge that will prove helpful along the way. But the changes that need to be made will have validity not because you heard that they are the latest trend, but because all those affected by what happens at your school had a voice and were participants, not spectators.

Early on in this book we suggested that an axis can be drawn distinguishing *authentic* from *bureaucratic* attempts to restructure schools. Authentic restructuring gets one closer to bedrock, and therefore deeper into the whole system itself. The idea of authenticity in restructuring is that it has about it a sense of integrity, of wholeness. Authentic restructuring comes from a desire to make a school a fundamentally good place. Bureaucratic restructuring, on the other hand, is a cynical process that involves such pursuits as tinkering with schedules, shuffling administrative assignments, and pasting on new labels and slogans without depth of character and commitment. As much as anything, it represents an attempt to create a sense of activity and progress when in fact there is no empirical evidence that improvement is taking place. Worse than that, bureaucratic restructuring leads to feelings of disillusion, and puts the schools in the position of the boy who cried wolf. In the children's story, a lonely, bored shepherd boy cried wolf in order to get attention even though there was no wolf. After the townspeople had responded to his false cries the first two times, they did not come to help him the third time when in fact there was a wolf.

The other axis we drew completes a quadrant when combined with the previous one. This second axis makes a distinction between restructuring efforts that are *participatory* versus those that are *mandated*. This distinction is very basic because it deals with the locus of control and whether that locus is internal and local or whether it is external and other-directed. To the extent that all those who will be affected by any attempt to restructure are actively involved in the process, the effort has validity. This is not to say that whatever people come up with locally is automatically good and that whatever is dictated to local people from central offices is automatically bad. Such reasoning brings confusion to the issue. We are attempting here to untangle the threads so that when they are woven together with care a better outcome will result.

Participation and ownership are empowering. They are fundamental to the work of a democratic society. We are saying the process must be democratic for it to be valid. The best ideas, imposed from outside, will never take root. They will always be an imposition. It is one thing for local folks to choose from a variety of alternative options put forth into the marketplace of ideas; it is yet another to impose ideas, no matter how great they are, on the people who must live with them.

WHAT SHOULD WE DO?

Recently, when we presented our findings on a wide range of educational innovations to a group of Texas administrators and teachers, a person in the audience raised his hand and asked sincerely, "What *should* we do?" It's a good question, but not one that is easily answered. Lao Tzu taught in the art of Zen that more often than we know it is advisable to do nothing. More recently, after the advent of talking pictures in the early 1930s, a famous director, exasperated by the wild gesturing of his actors whose training had been for silent movies where dramatic movement was the order of the day, screamed, "Don't just do something, stand there!"

Of course, we do not mean to imply that we endorse the status quo. Literally to "do nothing" would imply such an endorsement. What we mean to say is don't just do something simply because it is new or because it is sweeping the country. The Middle Way is found somewhere between being complacent on the one hand, and doing something in an attempt to create an image or illusion of progress on the other. But the answers are seldom found in the annals of sweeping changes based on castigating the old and praising the new. Whole new management protocols or changing the master schedule may yield little real difference even though they both represent major changes. Creating an atmosphere of intimacy and caring may yield substantial dividends even though no large grants or major sloganeering are necessary in order to bring about such a change.

Let us share some data from a national award-winning school restructuring effort for which we were outside evaluators. We were interested in compiling some "educational indicators" that are often overlooked as a means of testing whether progress is being made. In this particular school, one of the major changes was that of downsizing one portion of the faculty and student body of a school of 1500 students. This group became a school-within-the-school, and it had a student population of 78 students. One could speculate down the road to many such "schools" within the total structure, or perhaps to other permutations (*e.g.,* four "schools" of 375, etc.). But the point is very simple, and it should not be lost: simply create smaller structures that represent a more human scale. To test the hypothesis that a smaller scale will yield some meaningful differences, we compared the student profile of the "school-within-the-school" with a random selection of the same number of students from the student body at large. Here are a few of the findings:

	School-within-School	Other Students
Number of Full Days Absent	437	857
Average Days Absent	5.75	11.28
Percent of Students Referred for Disciplinary Reasons	12%	41%
Number of Truancy Notices	5	33
Percentage of Disciplinary Referrals to School Counselors	16%	41%

Having controlled for a host of other variables, we concluded that the dramatic differences between the two groups appears to support the hypothesis that more intimate surroundings do indeed make a difference, or to put things in more colloquial terms, results in a more "user-friendly" environment for young people. Take a moment to study the figures presented above. This is the kind of educational research data that practitioners can and should gather. It is at once simple and meaningful.

As far as we know, there is presently no shortage of gurus and "trainers" out there who are perfectly willing to tell and sell teachers and administrators what to do. But maybe one of the lessons that can come from this book and our previous book, *Research On Educational Innovations* (1993), is that what we should do is proceed thoughtfully, deliberately, and with caution. Change and progress, after all, are not necessarily the same thing.

REFERENCES

Bestor, A.E. (1953). *Educational Wastelands*. Urbana, IL: University of Illinois Press.

Conant, J.B. (1959). *The American High School Today: A First Report to Interested Citizens*. New York: McGraw-Hill.

Ellis, A.K., & Fouts, J.T. (1993). *Research on Educational Innovations*. Princeton Junction, NJ: Eye on Education.

Flesch, R. (1955). *Why Johnny Can't Read*. New York: Harper & Row.

Goodlad, J.I., & Anderson, R.H. (1959). *The Nongraded Elementary School*. New York: Teacher's College Press.

Goodlad, J.I. (1984). *A Place Called School: Prospects for the Future*. New York: McGraw-Hill.

Kuhn, T. (1970). *The Structure of Scientific Revolutions (2nd ed.)*. Chicago: University of Chicago Press.

Sarason, S.B. (1982). *The Culture of the School and the Problem of Change (2nd ed.)*. Boston: Allyn & Bacon.

Sarason, S.B. (1990). *The Predictable Failure of Educational Reform: Can We Change Course Before It's Too Late?* San Francisco: Jossey-Bass.

Sizer, T.R. (1986). Rebuilding: First steps by the Coalition of Essential Schools. *Phi Delta Kappan, 68(1)*, 38–42.

Wingo, G.M. (1965). *The Philosophy of American Education*, Boston: DC Heath and Company.

The scientific school establishment continues to float plans for further centralization in the form of national standards, a national curriculum, and improved national standardized testing. Magical promises are everywhere: machines are the answer; new forms of preschooling are the answer; baseball bats, bullhorns, and padlocks are the answer. In the face of a century and a half of searching for it unsuccessfully, nobody seems to doubt for a minute that there *is* an answer. One answer. The one right answer.

John Taylor Gatto

BIBLIOGRAPHY

CHAPTERS 1–4
GENERAL SOURCES ON SCHOOLS AND RESTRUCTURING

Adler, M.J., & The Paideia Group (1984). *The Paideia program: An educational syllabus.* New York: Macmillan.

American Association for the Advancement of Science (1989). *Science for all Americans: A Project 2061 report on literacy goals in science, mathematics, and technology.* Washington, DC: American Association for the Advancement of Science.

Bacharach, S.B. (ed.) (1990). *Education reform: Making sense of it all.* Boston: Allyn & Bacon.

Barth, R.S. (1990). *Improving schools from within: Teachers, parents, and principals can make the difference.* San Francisco: Jossey-Bass.

Bliss, J.R., Firestone, W.A., & Richards, C.E. (1991). *Rethinking effective schools: Research and practice.* Englewood Cliffs, NJ: Prentice-Hall.

Bonstingl, J.J. (1992). *Schools of quality: An introduction to total quality management in education.* Alexandria, VA: Association for Supervision and Curriculum Development.

Brandt, R. (ed.) (1990). Restructuring: What is it? *Educational Leadership, 47(7)* [entire issue].

Brandt, R. (ed.) (1991). Restructuring schools: What's really happening? *Educational Leadership, 48(8)* [entire issue].

Clune, W.H., & Witte, J.F. (eds.) (1990). *Choice and control in American education: Vol. 1. The theory of choice and control in American education.* Philadelphia: Falmer Press.

Clune, W.H. & Witte, J.F. (eds.) (1990). *Choice and control in American education: Vol. 1. The practice of choice, decentralization and school restructuring.* Philadelphia: Falmer Press.

Cohen, D.K., McLaughlin, M.W., & Talbert, J.E. (eds.) (1993). *Teaching for understanding: Challenges for policy and practice.* San Francisco: Jossey-Bass.

Coleman, J.S., & Hoffer, T. (1987). *Public and private high schools: The impact of communities.* New York: Basic Books.

Conley, D. (1991). *Restructuring schools: Educators adapt to a changing world.* Eugene, OR: University of Oregon, ERIC Clearinghouse on Educational Management.

Cuban, L. (1990). Reforming again, again, and again. *Educational Researcher, 19(1),* 3–13.

Darling-Hammond, L., & Ascher, C. (1991). *Creating accountability in big city schools.* New York: ERIC Clearinghouse on Urban Education, and National Center for Restructuring Education, Schools and Teaching.

David, J.L., Purkey, S., & White, P.A. (1989). *Restructuring in progress: Lessons from pioneering districts.* Washington, DC: National Governors' Association and University of Wisconsin-Madison, Center for Policy Research in Education.

Deal, T.E., & Peterson, K.D. (1990). *The principal's role in shaping school culture.* Washington, DC: U.S. Government Printing Office.

Elmore, R.F., & Associates (1990). *Restructuring schools: The next generation of educational reform.* San Francisco: Jossey-Bass.

Firestone, W.A., & Rosenblum, S. (1988). Building commitment in urban high schools. *Educational Evaluation and Policy Analysis, 10(4),* 285–99.

Fiske, E.B. (1991). *Smart schools, smart kids: Why do some schools work?* New York: Simon & Schuster.

Fuhrman, S.H. (ed.). (1993). *Designing coherent education policy: Improving the system.* San Francisco: Jossey-Bass.

Fuhrman, S., Clune, W.H., & Elmore, R.F. (1988). Research on educational reform: Lessons on the implementation of policy. *Teachers College Record, 90(2)*, 237–57.

Fuhrman, S.H., & Malen, B. (eds.). (1991). *The politics of curriculum and testing.* Philadelphia: Falmer Press.

Fullan, M.G. (1991). *The new meaning of educational change (2nd ed.).* New York: Teachers College Press.

Gardner, H. (1983). *Frames of mind: The theory of multiple intelligences.* New York: Basic Books.

Gardner, H. (1991). *The unschooled mind: How children think and how schools should teach.* New York: Basic Books.

Glickman, C.D. (1990). Pushing school reform to a new edge: The seven ironies of school empowerment. *Phi Delta Kappan, 72(1)*, 68–75.

Glickman, C.D. (1993). *Renewing America's schools: A guide for school-based action.* San Francisco: Jossey-Bass.

Goodlad, J.I. (1984). *A place called school: Prospects for the future.* New York: McGraw-Hill.

Greenfield, W. (ed.). (1987). *Instructional leadership: Concepts, issues, and controversies.* Boston: Allyn & Bacon.

Hess, G.A., Jr. (1991). *School restructuring, Chicago style.* Newbury Park, CA: Corwin.

Hill, P.T., Foster, G.E., & Gendler, T. (1990). *High schools with character.* Santa Monica: The RAND Corporation.

Hirsch, E.D., Jr. (1987). *Cultural literacy: What every American needs to know.* Boston: Houghton Mifflin.

Howard, E.R., & Keefe, J.W. (1991). *The CASE-IMS school improvement process.* Reston, VA: National Association of Secondary School Principals.

Johnson, S.M. (1990). *Teachers at work: Achieving success in our schools.* New York: Basic Books.

Johnson, D.W., & Johnson, R.T. (1975). *Learning together and alone: Cooperation, competition and individualization.* Englewood Cliffs, NJ: Prentice-Hall.

Keffe, J.W., Jenkins, J.M., & Hersey, P.W. (eds.). (1992). *A leader's guide to school restructuring.* Reston, VA: National Association of Secondary School Principals.

Kozol, J. (1991). *Savage inequalities: Children in America's schools.* New York: Crown.

Levine, M., & Trachtman, R. (1988). *American business and the public school: Case studies of corporate involvement in public education.* New York: Committee for Economic Development.

Lewis, A. (1989). *Restructuring America's schools.* Arlington, VA: American Association of School Administrators.

Lieberman, A., & Miller, L. (1990). Restructuring schools: What matters and what works. *Phi Delta Kappan, 71(10),* 759–64.

Lieberman, A. (ed.). (1986). *Rethinking school improvement: Research, craft, and concept.* New York: Teachers College Press.

Livingston, C. (1992). *Teachers as leaders: Evolving roles.* Washington, DC: National Education Association.

Louis, K.S., & Miles, M.B. (1990). *Improving the urban high school: What works and why.* New York: Teachers College Press.

MacIver, D.J., & Epstein, J.L. (1992). Middle grades education: Middle schools and junior high schools. *Encyclopedia of Educational Research (6th ed.).* New York: Macmillan, 834–44.

Manasse, A.L. (1985). Improving conditions for principal effectiveness: Policy implications of research. *The Elementary School Journal, 85(3),* 138–62.

Marshall, H.H. (ed.). (1992). *Redefining student learning: Roots of educational change.* Norwood, NJ: Ablex.

Marzano, R.J., Brandt, R.S., Hughes, C.S., Jones, B.F., Presseisen, B.Z., Rankin, S.C., & Suhor, C. (1988). *Dimensions of thinking: A framework for curriculum and instruction.* Alexandria, VA: Association for Supervision and Curriculum Development.

McLaughlin, M.W., & Talbert, J., with Kahne, J., & Powell, J. (1990). Constructing a personalized school environment. *Phi Delta Kappan, 72(3),* 230–35.

McLaughlin, M., Talbert, J.E., & Bascia, N. (eds.). (1990). *The context of teachers' work in secondary schools.* New York: Teachers College Press.

Metz, M.H. (1986). *Different by design: The context and character of three magnet schools.* New York: Routledge & Kegan Paul.

Murphy, J. (1990). Principal instructional leadership. In P.W. Thurston & L.S. Lotto (eds.), *Advances in educational administration: Vol. 1, Part B. Changing perspectives on the school.* Greenwich, CT: JAI Press, 163–200.

Murphy, J. (1991). *Restructuring schools: Capturing and assessing the phenomena.* New York: Teachers College Press.

Murphy, J. (1992). Restructuring America's schools: An overview. In C.E. Finn, Jr., & T. Rebarber (eds.), *Education reform in the 90s.* New York: Macmillan, 3–20.

Murphy, J., & Hallinger, P. (eds.). (1993). *Restructuring schooling: Learning from ongoing efforts.* Newbury Park, CA: Corwin.

National Alliance of Business (1989). *A blueprint for business on restructuring education.* Washington, DC: National Alliance of Business.

National Commission on Excellence in Education (1983). *A nation at risk.* Washington, DC: U.S. Government Printing Office.

National Governors' Association (1989). *From rhetoric to action: State progress in restructuring the education system.* Washington, DC: National Governors' Association.

Newmann, F.M. (1991). Linking restructuring to authentic student achievement. *Phi Delta Kappan, 72(6),* 458–63.

Newmann, F.M. (1993). Beyond common sense in educational restructuring: The issues of content and linkage. *Educational Researcher, (22)2,* 4–13, 22.

Norris, S.P. (ed.) (1992). *The generalizability of critical thinking: Multiple perspectives on an educational ideal.* New York: Teachers College Press.

Pallas, A.M. (1988). School climate in American high schools. *Teachers College Record, 89(4),* 541–54.

Powell, A.G., Farrar, E., & Cohen, D.K. (1985). *The shopping mall high school: Winners and losers in the educational marketplace.* Boston: Houghton Mifflin.

Ratzki, A., & Fisher, A. (1989/90). Life in a restructured school. *Educational Leadership, 47(4),* 46–51.

Reyes, P. (ed.) (1990). *Teachers and their workplace: Commitment, performance and productivity.* San Francisco: Sage.

Rosenholtz, S.J. (1991). *Teachers' workplace: The social organization of schools.* New York: Teachers College Press.

Sarason, S.B. (1990). *The predictable failure of educational reform: Can we change course before it's too late?* San Francisco: Jossey-Bass.

Schlechty, P.C. (1990). *Schools for the 21st century: Leadership imperatives for educational reform.* San Francisco: Jossey-Bass.

Seeley, D.S. (1985). *Education through partnership*. Washington DC: American Enterprise Institute for Public Policy Research.

Shanker, A. (1990). The end of the traditional model of schooling—and a proposal for using incentives to restructure our public schools. *Phi Delta Kappan, 71(5)*, 344–57.

Shanker, A., & Rosenberg, B. (1991, Winter). *Politics, markets and America's schools: The fallacies of private school choice*. Washington, DC: American Federation of Teachers.

Shedd, J.B., & Bacharach, S.B. (1991). *Tangled hierarchies: Teachers as professionals and the management of schools*. San Francisco: Jossey-Bass.

Sizer, T.R. (1992). *Horace's School: Redesigning the American high school*. Boston: Houghton Mifflin.

Sizer, T.R. (1984). *Horace's Compromise: The dilemma of the American high school*. Boston: Houghton Mifflin.

Smith, M.S., O'Day, J., & Cohen, D.K. (1990). National curriculum American style: Can it be done? What might it look like? *American Educator, 14(4)*, 10–17, 40–47.

Stevenson, H.W., & Stigler, J.W. (1992). *The learning gap: Why our schools are failing and what we can learn from Japanese and Chinese education*. New York: Summit Books.

Wheelock, A. (1992). *Crossing the tracks: How "untracking" can save America's schools*. New York: The New Press.

CHAPTER 5
OUTCOME-BASED EDUCATION

Block, J.J., Efthim, H.E., & Burns, R.B. (1989). *Building effective mastery learning schools*. New York: Longman.

Bloom, B.S (1984). The search for methods of group instruction as effective as one-to-one tutoring. *Educational Leadership, 41(8)*, 4–17.

Brandt, R. (1992/93). On outcome-based education: A conversation with Bill Spady. *Educational Leadership, 50(4)*, 66–70.

Burns, R., & Squires, D. (1987). Curriculum organization in outcome-based education. *The OBE Bulletin, 3.* San Francisco, CA: Far West Laboratory for Educational Research and development (ERIC Document Reproduction Service No. ED294313).

Carroll, J.B. (1963). A model for school learning. *Teachers College Record, 64,* 723–33.

Erickson, W., Valdez, G., & McMillan, W. (1990). *Outcome-based education.* St. Paul, MN: Minnesota Department of Education.

Guskey, T.R., & Gates, S.L. (1986). Synthesis of research on the effects of mastery learning in elementary and secondary classrooms. *Educational Leadership, 43(8),* 73–81.

Guskey, T.R., & Pigott, T.D. (1988). Research on group-based mastery learning programs: A meta-analysis. *Journal of Educational Research, 81(4),* 197–216.

Guskey, T.R. Rethinking mastery learning reconsidered. *Review of Educational Research, 57(2),* 225–29.

Kulik, C.C., & Kulik, J. (1986/87). Mastery testing and student learning: A meta-analysis." *Journal of Educational Technology Systems, 15(3),* 325–41.

McKernan, J. (1993). Some limitations of outcome-based education. *Journal of Curriculum Studies, 8(4),* 343–53.

Murphy, C. (ed.) (1984). *Outcome-Based Instructional Systems: Primer and Practice. Education Brief.* San Francisco, CA: Far West Laboratory for Educational Research and Development (ERIC Document Reproduction Service No. ED249265).

Network for Outcome-Based Schools. *Outcomes* (quarterly publication of the Network). Johnson City, NY: Johnson City Central Schools.

Rubin, S.E., & Spady, W. (1984). Achieving excellence through outcome based instructional delivery. *Educational Leadership, 41(8),* 37–44.

Slavin, R.E. (1987). Mastery learning reconsidered. *Review of Educational Research, 57(2),* 175–213.

Spady, W.G. (1988). Organizing for results: The basis of authentic restructuring and reform. *Educational Leadership, 46(2),* 4–8.

Spady, W.G. (1981). *Outcome-Based Instructional Management: A Sociological Perspective.* Washington, DC: National Institute of Education (ERIC Document Reproduction Service No. ED 244728).

Spady, W.G. (1991). Beyond traditional outcome-based education. *Educational Leadership, 49(2),* 67–72.

Stallings, J., & Stipek, D. (1986). Research on early childhood and elementary school teaching programs. In M.C. Witrock (ed.), *Handbook of Research on Teaching (3rd ed.).* New York: Macmillan.

Stephens, G.M., & Herman, J.J. (1984). Outcome-based educational planning. *Educational Leadership, 41(8),* 45–47.

Vickery, T.R. (1990). ODDM: A workable model for total school improvement. *Educational Leadership, 47(7),* 67–70.

Walberg, H.J. (1984). Improving the productivity of America's schools. *Educational Leadership, 41(8),* 19–27.

Walberg, H. (1985) Examining the theory, practice, and outcomes of mastery learning. In D.U. Levine (ed.), *Improving student achievement through mastery learning programs.* San Francisco, CA: Jossey-Bass.

Chapter 6
Site-Based Management

Brown, D.J. (1990). *Decentralization and school-based management.* New York: Falmer Press.

Cawelti, G. (1989). Key elements of site-based management. *Educational Leadership, 46(8),* 46.

Chion-Kennedy, L. (1987). The Coalition of Essential Schools: A report from the field. *American Educator, 11(4),* 47–48.

Conley, S. (1991). Review of research on teacher participation in school decisionmaking. In G. Grant (ed.), *Review of research in education: Vol. 17.* Washington, DC: American Educational Research Association, 225–65.

Conley, S., & Bacharach, S. (1990). From school-site management to participatory school-site management. *Phi Delta Kappan, 71(7),* 539–44.

Cotton, K. (1992). *School-based management (Topical Synthesis #6).* Portland, OR: Northwest Regional Educational Laboratory.

David, J.L. (1989). Synthesis of research on school-based management. *Educational Leadership, 46(9),* 45–53.

Glickman, C.D. (1993). Restructuring policy for America's schools. *NASSP Bulletin, 76(549),* 87–97.

Glickman, C.D. (1990). Pushing school reform to a new edge: The seven ironies of school empowerment. *Phi Delta Kappan, 72(1),* 68–75.

Goldman, P., Dunlap, D.M., & Conley, D.T. (1993). Facilitative power and nonstandardized solutions to school site restructuring. *Educational Administration Quarterly, 29(1),* 69–92.

Harrison, C.R., Killion, J.P., & Mitchell, J.E. (1989). Site-based management: The realities of implementation. *Educational Leadership, 46(8),* 55–58.

Hill, P., & Bonan, J. (1991). *Decentralization and accountability in public education.* Santa Monica, CA: The RAND Corporation.

Kliebard, H.M. (1986). *The Struggle for the American Curriculum: 1893–1958.* Boston: Routledge and Kegan Paul.

Lane, J.J., & Epps, E.G. (eds.). (1992). *Restructuring the schools: Problems and prospects.* Berkeley, CA: McCutchan.

Lange, J.T. (1993). Site-based, shared decisionmaking: A resource for restructuring. *NASSP Bulletin* (January), 98–107.

Lieberman, A., Zuckerman, D., Wilkie, A., Smith, E., Barinas, N., & Hergert, L. (1991). *Early lessons in restructuring schools: Case studies of schools of tomorrow . . . today.* New York: National Center for Restructuring Education, Schools, and Teaching, Columbia University.

McGregor, D.M. (1960). *The Human Side of Enterprise.* New York: McGraw-Hill Book Company.

Owens, R.G. (1991). *Organizational Behavior in Education (4th ed.).* Englewood Cliffs, NJ: Prentice Hall.

Peterson, D. (1991). *School-Based Management and Student Performance.* University of Oregon: Clearinghouse on Educational Management (ERIC Digest No. 62).

Taylor, B.O., & Levine, D.U. (1991). Effective schools projects and school-based management. *Phi Delta Kappan, 72(5),* 394–97.

Wood, F.H., & Caldwell, S.D. (1991). Planning and training to implement site-based management. *Journal of Staff Development, 12(3),* 25–29.

Chapter 7
Total Quality Management (TQM)

Argyris, C. (1957). *Personality and organization: The conflict between the system and the individual.* New York: Harper & Row.

Bonstingl, J.J. (1992). *Schools of quality: An introduction to total quality management in education.* Alexandria, VA: Association for Supervision and Curriculum Development.

Bonstingl, J.J. (1992). The quality revolution in education. *Educational Leadership, 50(3),* 4–9.

Brandt, R. (ed.) (1992). *Educational Leadership, 50(3)* [entire issue].

Bruner, J.S. (1966). *The Process of education.* New York: Vintage Books.

Capper C.A., & Jamison, M.T. (1993). Let the buyer beware: Total quality management and educational research and practice. *Educational Researcher, 22(8),* 15–30.

Crawford, D.K., Bodine, R.J., & Hoglund, R.C. (1993). *The school for quality learning.* Champaign, Illinois: Research Press.

Deming, W.E. (1993). *The new economics for industry, government, and education.* Cambridge, MA: MIT Center for Advanced Engineering Study.

Glasser, W. (1990). *The quality school.* New York: Harper & Row.

Glasser, W. (1965). *Reality therapy.* New York: Harper & Row.

Holt, M. (1993). The educational consequences of W. Edwards Deming. *Phi Delta Kappan* (January), 382–88.

Leading indicators—Assorted facts and opinions for recent research on American education. (1992, Spring). *Agenda: America's Schools for the 21st Century.*

Likert, R. *New patterns of management.* New York: McGraw-Hill.

Macchia, P., Jr. (1992). Total quality education and instructional systems development. *Educational Technology, 32(7),* 17–20.

McCormick, B.L. (ed.) (1993). *Quality and education: Critical linkages.* Princeton Junction, NJ: Eye on Education.

McGregor, D.M. (1960). *The human side of enterprise.* New York: McGraw-Hill Book Company.

Melvin, C.A. (1991). Restructuring schools by applying Deming's management theories. *Journal of Staff Development, 12(3)*, 16–20.

Owens, R.G. (1991). *Organizational behavior in education (4th ed.)*. Englewood Cliffs, NJ: Prentice Hall.

Rankin, S.C. (1992). Total quality management: Implications for educational assessment. *NASSP Bulletin, 76(545)*, 66–76.

Schmoker, M., & Wilson, R. (1993). Transforming schools through total quality education. *Phi Delta Kappan, 74(5)*, 389–95.

Sztajin, P. (1992). A matter of metaphors: Education as a handmade process. *Educational Leadership, 50(3)*, 35–37.

Walton, M. (1986). *The Deming management method*. New York: Perigee.

CHAPTER 8
YEAR-ROUND SCHOOLS

Ballinger, C. (1993). *Annual report to the association on the status of year-round education.* San Diego, CA: National Association for Year-Round Education (ERIC Document Reproduction Service No. ED358551).

Bradford, J.C. (1991). *Year-round schools: A national perspective.* Franklin, VA: Franklin City Public Schools (ERIC Document Reproduction Service No. ED343259).

Bradford, J.C. (1992). *A national model: A voluntary four-quarter plan at the high school Level.* Buena Vista, VA: Buena Vista Public Schools (ERIC Document Reproduction Service No. ED343261).

Brekke, N.R. (1990). *YRE: A break from tradition that makes educational and economic sense.* Oxnard, CA: Oxnard School District (ERIC Document Reproduction Service No. ED324818).

Gandara, P. (1992). Extended year, extended contracts: Increasing teacher salary options. *Urban Education, 27(3)*, 229–47.

Herman, J.L. (1991). Novel approaches to relieve overcrowding: The effects of Concept 6 year-round schools. *Urban Education, 26(2)*, 195–213.

Howell, V. (1988). *An examination of YRE: Pros and cons that challenge schooling in America.* (ERIC Document Reproduction Service No. ED298602)

National Commission on Excellence in Education (1983). *A nation at risk.* Washington, DC: U.S. Government Printing Office.

National Education Association (1987). *Year-round schools. "What research says about:"* Washington, DC: National Education Association (ERIC Document Reproduction Service No. ED310486).

Peltier, G.L. (1991). Year-round education: The controversy and research evidence. *NASSP Bulletin, 75(536),* 120–29.

Rasberry, Q. (1992). *Year-round schools may not be the answer.* (ERIC Document Reproduction Service No. ED353658).

White, W.D. (1992). Year-round no more. *American School Board Journal, 178(7),* 27–30.

Zykowski, J. (1991). *A Review of Year-Round Education Research.* Riverside, CA: California Educational Research Cooperative (ERIC Document Reproduction Service No. ED330040).

CHAPTER 9
PARENTAL INVOLVEMENT

Berger, E.H. (1991). Parent involvement: Yesterday and today. *Elementary School Journal, 91(3),* 209–19.

Brandt, R. (ed.) (1989). Strengthening partnerships with parents and community: *Educational Leadership, 47(2)* [entire issue].

Chicago Public Schools, Office of Reform (1993). *LSC sourcebook: Basics for the Local School Councils.* Chicago: Board of Education of the City of Chicago.

Cotton, K., & Wikelund, K.R. (1989). *Parent involvement in education.* Portland, OR: Northwest Regional Educational Laboratory.

Dixon, A.P. (1992). Parents: Full partnership in the decision-making process. *NASSP Bulletin, 76(543),* 15–18.

Epstein, J.L. (1992). School and family partnerships. In M.C. Alkin (ed.), *Encyclopedia of Educational Research (6th ed.).* New York: MacMillan, 1139–51.

Hess, G.A., Jr. (1991). *Chicago and Britain: Experiments in empowering parents. The second wave of reform: Restructuring schools.* (ERIC Document Reproduction Service No. ED334664).

Lareau, A. (1989). *Home advantage: Social class and parental intervention in elementary education.* New York: Falmer Press.

McLaughlin, M.W., & Shields, P.M. (1987). Involving low income parents in the schools: A role for policy? *Phi Delta Kappan, 69(2)*, 156–60.

Maeroff, G.I. (1992). Reform comes home: Policies to encourage parental involvement in children's education. In C.E. Finn, Jr., & T. Rebarber (eds.), *Education reform in the 90's.* New York: Macmillan, 155–71.

Moles, O.C. (1982). Synthesis of recent research on parent participation in children's education. *Educational Leadership, 40(2)*, 44–47.

North Central Regional Educational Laboratory (1993). *Integrating community services for young children and their families (Policy Briefs, Report 3).* Oak Brook, IL: North Central Regional Educational Laboratory.

Northwest Regional Educational Laboratory (1990). *Effective schooling practices: A research synthesis 1990 update.* Portland, OR: Northwest Regional Educational Laboratory.

Rioux, J.W., & Berla, N. (1993). *Innovations in parent & family involvement.* Princeton Junction, NJ: Eye on Education.

Stevenson, H. (1992). Learning from Asian schools. *Scientific American, 267(6)*, 70–76.

Walberg, H. (1984). Improving the productivity of America's schools. *Educational Leadership, 41(8)*, 19–27.

Wang, M.C., Haertel, G.D., & Walberg, H. (1993). Toward a knowledge base for school learning. *Review of Educational Research, 63(3)*, 249–94.

Wang, M.C., Haertel, G.D., & Walberg, H. (1993/94). What helps students learn? *Educational Leadership, 51(4)*, 74–79.

Williams, D.L., & Chavkin, N.F. (1989). Essential elements of strong parent involvement programs. *Educational Leadership, 47(2)*, 18–20.

Young, R.E. (1990). *A critical theory of education: Habermas and our children's future.* New York: Teacher's College Press.

CHAPTER 10
EDUCATIONAL CHOICE

Bastian, A. (1992). Which choice? Whose choice? *Clearing House,* *66(2),* 96–99.

Chubb, J.E., & Moe, T.M. (1990). *Politics, markets, and America's schools.* Washington, DC: The Brookings Institute.

Coons, J.E., & Sugarman, S.D. (1991). The private school option in systems of educational choice. *Educational Leadership,* *48(4),* 54–56.

Corwin, T.M. (1992). Introduction: Examining school choice issues. *Clearing House, 66(2),* 68–70.

Elam, S.M. (1990). The 22nd Annual Gallop Poll of the public's attitudes toward the public schools. *Phi Delta Kappan, 72(1),* 41–55.

Farnan, P. (1993). A choice for Etta Wallace. *Policy Review, 64(2),* 24–27.

Glazier, N. (1993). American public education: The relevance of choice. *Phi Delta Kappan, 74(8),* 647–50.

Hayes, L. (1992) A simple matter of humanity: An interview with Jonathan Kozol. *Phi Delta Kappan, 74(4),* 334–37.

James, T., & Levin, H.M. (1988). *Comparing public and private schools: Vol. 1. Institutions and organizations.* Philadelphia: Falmer Press.

Kozol, J. (1991). *Savage inequalities: Children in America's schools.* New York: Crown.

Kozol, J. (1992a). I dislike the idea of choice, and I want to tell you why. *Educational Leadership, 50(3),* 90–92.

Kozol, J. (1992b). Flaming folly. *Executive Educator, 14(6),* 14–19.

Mulholland, L., & Amsler, M. (1992). *The search for choice in public education: The emergence of charter schools.* San Francisco: Far West Laboratory for Educational Research and Development (ERIC Document Reproduction Service No. ED354583).

Sautter, R.C. (1993). *Charter schools: A new breed of public schools.* Oakbrook, IL: North Central Regional Educational Laboratory.

Strate, J.M., & Wilson, C.A. (1991). *Schools of choice in the Detroit metropolitan area.* Detroit: Center for Urban Studies, Wayne State University (ERIC Document Reproduction Service No. ED355287).

CHAPTER 11
INSTRUCTIONAL GROUPING ALTERNATIVES

Allan, S.D. (1991). Ability-Grouping research reviews: What do they say about grouping and the gifted? *Educational Leadership, 48(6),* 60–65.

Ansah, V. (1989). *Multiage grouping and academic achievement.* (ERIC Document Reproduction Service No. ED315163).

Brandt, R. (ed.) (1992). Untracking for equity. *Educational Leadership, 50(2)* [entire issue].

Cotton, K. (1993). *Nongraded primary education.* Portland, OR: Northwest Regional Educational Laboratory.

Ford, B.E. (1977). Multiage grouping in the elementary school and children's affective development: A review of recent research. *The Elementary School Journal, 78(2),* 149–59.

Gamoran, A. (1987). The stratification of high school learning opportunities. *Sociology of Education, 60(3),* 135–55.

Gamoran, A. (1992). Is ability grouping equitable? *Educational Leadership, 50(2),* 11–17.

Gamoran, A., & Berends, M. (1987). The effects of stratification in secondary schools: Synthesis of survey and ethnographic research. *Review of Educational Research, 57(4),* 415–35.

Goodlad, J.I., & Anderson, R.H. (1987). *The nongraded elementary school. Revised edition.* New York: Teacher's College Press.

Guitierrez, R., & Slavin, R. (1992). Achievement effects of the nongraded elementary school: A best-evidence synthesis. *Review of Educational Research, 62(4),* 333–76.

Hallinan, M. (1990). The effects of ability grouping in secondary schools: A response to Slavin's best evidence synthesis. *Review of Educational Research, 60(3),* 501–04.

Kilgore, S.B. (1991). The organizational context of tracking in schools. *American Sociological Review, 56,* 189–203.

Kulik, J.A. (1991). Findings on grouping are often distorted. *Educational Leadership, 48(6),* 67.

Kulik, J.A. (1992). *An analysis of the research on ability grouping: Historical and contemporary perspectives.* Storrs, CT: The National Research Center on the Gifted and Talented.

Kulik, C.L., & Kulik, J.A. (1984). *Effects of ability grouping on elementary school pupils: A meta-analysis.* Paper presented at the 92nd Annual Meeting of the American Psychological Association, Aug. 24–28, 1984, Toronto, Canada (ERIC Document Reproduction Service No. ED255329).

Kulik, C.L., & Kulik, J.A. (1987). Effects of ability grouping on student achievement. *Equity and Excellence, 23(1),* 22–30.

McGurk, E.K., & Pimentle, J.A. (1992). *Alternative instructional grouping practices.* (ERIC Document Reproduction Service No. ED353279).

McLaughlin, M.W., & Talbert, J. (1990). Constructing a personalized school environment. *Phi Delta Kappan, 72(3),* 230–35.

Miller, B.A. (1990). A review of the quantitative research on multigrade instruction. *Research in Rural Education, 7(1),* 1–8.

Miller, B.A. (1991). A review of the qualitative research on multigrade instruction. *Research in Rural Education, 7(2),* 3–12.

Murphy, J., & Hallinger, P. (1989). Equity as access to learning: Curricular and instructional treatment differences. *Journal of Curriculum Studies, 21(2),* 129–49.

Natriello, G., Pallas, A.M., & Alexander, K. (1989). On the right track? Curriculum and academic achievement. *Sociology of Education, 62(2),* 109–18.

Northwest Regional Educational Laboratory (1990). *Effective Schooling Practices: A Research Synthesis 1990 Update.* Portland, OR: Northwest Regional Educational Laboratory.

Oxley, D. (1994). Organizing schools into small units: Alternatives to homogenous grouping. *Phi Delta Kappan, 75(7),* 521–26.

Page, R.N. (1991). *Lower Track classrooms: A circular and cultural perspective.* New York: Teachers College Press.

Pavan, B.N. (1977). The nongraded elementary school: research on academic achievement and mental health. *Texas Tech Journal of Education, 4(2),* 91–107.

Pavan, B.N. (1992). The benefits of nongraded schools. *Educational Leadership, 50(2),* 22–25.

Pratt, D. (1986). On the merits of multiage classrooms. Their work life. *Research in Rural Education, 3(3),* 111–16.

Sharan, S. (ed.). (1990). *Cooperative learning: Theory and research.* New York: Praeger.

Slavin, R. (1987). Ability grouping and student achievement in elementary schools: A best-evidence synthesis. *Review of Educational Research, 57(3),* 293–336.

Slavin, R. (1990). Achievement effects of ability grouping in secondary schools: A best-evidence synthesis. *Review of Educational Research, 60(3),* 471–99.

Slavin, R. (1993). Ability grouping in the middle grades: Achievement effects and alternatives. *Elementary School Journal, 93(5),* 535–52.

Sorensen, A.B., & Hallinan, M.T. (1986). Effects of ability grouping on growth in academic achievement. *American Educational Research Journal, 23(4),* 519–42.

Wheelock, A. (1992). *Crossing the tracks: How "untracking" can save America's schools.* New York: The New Press.

CHAPTER 12
ALTERNATIVE ASSESSMENT

Applebee, A.N., Langer, J.A., & Mullis, I.V.S. (1989). *Understanding direct writing assessments.* Princeton, NJ: Educational Testing Service.

Archbald, D., & Newmann, F.M. (1988). *Beyond standardized testing: Assessing authentic academic achievement in the secondary school.* Reston, VA: National Association of Secondary School Principals.

Berlak, H., Newmann, F.M., Adams, E., Archbald, D.A., Burgess, T., Raven, J., & Romberg, T. (1992). *Toward a new science of educational testing and assessment.* Albany, NY: State University of New York.

Brandt, R. (ed.) (1992). *Readings from Educational Leadership: Performance assessment.* Alexandria, VA: Association for Supervision and Curriculum Development.

Brandt, R. (ed.) (1992). Using performance assessment. *Educational Leadership, 49(8)* [entire issue].

Cronin, J.F. (1993). Four misconceptions about authentic learning. *Educational Leadership, 50(7),* 78–80.

Ellis, A.K. (1991). Evaluation as problemsolving. *Curriculum in Context, 19(2),* 30–31.

Herman, J.L., Aschbacher, P.R., & Winters, L. (1992). *A practical guide to alternative assessment.* Alexandria, VA: Association for Supervision and Curriculum Development.

Lehman, N. (1994). Is there a science of success? *The Atlantic Monthly, 273(2),* 83–98.

Mitchell, R. (1992). *Testing for learning: How new approaches to evaluation can improve American schools.* New York: Free Press.

National Council on Educational Standards and Testing (1992). *Raising standards for American education.* Washington, DC: U.S. Government Printing Office.

Newmann, F.M., & Wehlage, G.G. (1993). Five standards of authentic instruction. *Educational Leadership, 50(7),* 8–12.

Perrone, V. (1991). *Expanding student assessment.* Alexandria, VA: Association for Supervision and Curriculum Development.

Rayborn, R. (1992). Alternatives for assessing student achievement: Let me count the ways. In *Assessment: How Do We Know What They Know?.* Union, WA: Washington State Association for Supervision and Curriculum Development, 24–27.

Toch, T. (1991). *In the name of excellence: The struggle to reform the nation's schools and why it's failing and what should be done.* New York: Oxford University Press.

Wiggins, G. (1989). The futility of trying to teach everything of importance. *Educational Leadership, 47(3),* 44–59.

Wiggins, G. (1989). A true test: Toward more authentic and equitable assessment. *Phi Delta Kappan, 70(9),* 703–14.

Wiggins, G. (1989). Teaching to the (authentic) test. *Educational Leadership, 46(7),* 41–47.

Wiggins, G. (1991). Standards, not standardization: Evoking quality student work. *Educational Leadership, 48(5),* 18–25.

Wiggins, G. (1992). Creating tests worth taking. *Educational Leadership, 49(8),* 26–33.

Worthen, B.R. (1993). Critical issues that will determine the future of alternative assessment. *Phi Delta Kappan, 74(6),* 444–48.

CHAPTER 13
EDUCATIONAL TECHNOLOGY

Adams, S., & Bailey, G. (1993). Education for the information age: Is it time to trade vehicles? *NASSP Bulletin, 77(553),* 57–63.

Bender, P.V. (1991). The effectiveness of integrated computer learning systems in the elementary school. *Contemporary Education, 63(1),* 19–23.

Becker, H.J. (1987). *The impact of computer use on children's learning: What research has shown and what it has not.* Paper presented at the Annual Meeting of the American Educational Research Association, April 20–24, 1987, Washington, DC (ERIC Document Reproduction Service No. ED287458).

Bracey, G. (1988). Computers and learning: The research jury is still out. *Electronic Learning, 8(2),* 28, 30.

Braun, L. (1993). Educational technology: Help for all the kids. *The Computing Teacher, 20(8),* 11–15.

Clark, R.E. (1983). Reconsidering research on learning from media. *Review of Educational Research, 53(4),* 445–59.

Clark, R.E. (1985). Evidence for confounding in computer-based instruction studies: Analyzing the meta-analysis. *Educational Communication and Technology, 33(4),* 249–62.

Clark, R.E. (1985). Confounding in educational computing research. *Journal of Educational Computing Research, 1(2),* 137–48.

Clark, R.E. (1991). When researchers swim upstream: Reflections on an unpopular argument about learning from media. *Educational Technology, 31(2),* 34–40.

Clark, R.E. (1992). Dangers in the evaluation of instructional media. *Academic Medicine, 67(12),* 819–20.

Cotton, K. (1991). *Computer-Assisted Instruction.* Portland, OR: Northwest Regional Educational Laboratory.

Educational Leadership (1994), *51(7)* [entire issue].

Hannafin, R.D., & Savenye, W.C. (1993). Technology in the classroom: The teacher's new role and resistance to it. *Educational Technology, 33(6)*, 26–31.

Knapp, L., & Glenn, A. (1994). *Restructuring schools with technology.* Boston: Allyn & Bacon, Simon & Schuster Education Group.

Kozma, R.B. (1991). Learning with media. *Review of Educational Research, 61(2)*, 179–211.

Kulik, J.E., & Kulik, C.L. (1987). *Computer-based instruction: What 200 evaluations say.* Ann Arbor, MI: Center for Research on Learning and Teaching, University of Michigan (ERIC Document Reproduction Service No. ED285521).

Kulik, C.L., & Kulik, J.A. (1991). Effectiveness of computer-based instruction: An updated analysis. *Computers in Human Behavior, 7(1–2)*, 75–94.

Liao, Y.K. (1992). Effects of computer-assisted instruction on cognitive outcomes: A meta-analysis. *Journal of Research on Computing in Education, 24(3)*, 367–80.

McNeil, B.J., & Nelson, K.R. (1991). Meta-analysis of interactive video instruction: A 10-year review of achievement effects. *Journal of Computer-Based Instruction, 18(1)*, 1–6.

Newman, D. (Dec., 1992). Technology as support for school structure and school restructuring. *Phi Delta Kappan, 74(4)*, 308–15.

Niemiec, R., Weinstein, T., & Walberg, H.J. (1987). The effects of computer-based instruction in elementary schools: A quantitative synthesis. *Journal of Research on Computing in Education, 20(2)*, 85–103.

Papert, S. (1980). *Mindstorms: Children, computers and powerful ideas.* New York: Basic Books.

Papert, S. (1993). *Children's machines.* New York: Basic Books.

Roblyer, M.D. (1988). The effectiveness of microcomputers in education: A review of the research from 1980–1987. *Technological Horizons in Education Journal, 16(2)*, 85–89.

Ryan, A.W. (1991). Meta-analysis of achievement effects of microcomputer applications in elementary schools. *Educational Administration Quarterly, 27(2)*, 161–84.

Sullivan, H.J., Igoe, A.R., Klein, J.D., Jones, E.E., & Savanye, W.C. (1993). Perspectives on the future of educational technology. *Educational Technology Research & Development, 41(2)*, 97–110.

CHAPTER 14
COOPERATIVE LEARNING

Aronson, E., Blaney, N., Stephan, C., Sikes, J., & Snapp, M. (1978). *The jigsaw classroom.* Beverly Hills, CA: Sage.

Deutsch, M. (1949). A theory of cooperation and competition. *Human Relations, 2,* 129–52.

Johnson, D., Johnson, R., & Holubec, E. (1988). *Cooperation in the classroom.* Edina, MN: Interaction Book Company.

Johnson, D.W., & Johnson, R.T. (1988). *Leading the cooperative school.* Edina, MN: Interaction Book Company.

Johnson, D., & Johnson, R. (1989). *Cooperation and competition: Theory and research.* Edina, MN: Interaction Book Company.

Johnson, D., & Johnson, R. (1994). *Leading the cooperative school, 2nd ed.* Edina, MN: Interaction Book Company.

Kagan, S. (1989). *Cooperative learning resources for teachers.* San Juan Capistrano, CA: Resources for Teachers.

Kagan, S. (1989/90). The structural approach to cooperative learning. *Educational Leadership, 47(4),* 12–16.

Lewin, K. (1947). *Field theory in social sciences.* New York: Harper & Row.

Slavin, R. (1991). Synthesis of research on cooperative learning. *Educational Leadership, 48(5),* 71–82.

Slavin, R. (1989/90). Research on cooperative learning: Consensus and controversy. *Educational Leadership, 47(4),* 52–54.

Slavin, R. (1989/90). Here to stay—or gone tomorrow. *Educational Leadership, 47(4),* 3.

Slavin, R. (1986). *Educational Psychology: Theory into Practice.* Englewood Cliffs, NJ: Prentice-Hall.

Slavin, R., et al., (eds.) (1985). *Learning to cooperate, cooperating to learn.* New York: Plenum Press.

INDEX

ability grouping 147,
   150–51, 159
Adams, S. 177, 181, 183, 190
age-graded classrooms
   150–51
agrarian calendar 99
Allan, S. 158, 160
alternative assessment
   163–76, 211
America 2000 Goals 94
Amsler, M. 140–41, 145
Anderson, R. 152, 156, 160,
212, 224
Ansah, V. 157, 160
apprenticeships 217
Argyris, C. 78, 95
Aronson, E. 198, 199, 204
audio-visual instruction 179
authentic assessment 167–69

Bagley, W. 3
Bailey, G. 177, 181, 183, 190
Ballinger, C. 101, 105, 108
bandwagons 91
Bastian, A. 144
Becker, H. 189, 190

behavioral objectives 30
Bennett, W. 123, 125
Berla, N. 111, 117, 119, 126
Bestor, A. 211, 223
Bloom, B. 41, 58, 63, 65
Bodine, R 90, 95, 97
Bonstingl, J. 95, 97
Bradford, J. 99, 104, 105,
   107, 109
Brandt, R. 53–54, 65, 118
Braun, L. 177, 181, 189
Brekke, N. 99
Brophy, J. 41
*Brown vs the Board of
   Education* 213
Bruner, J. 41, 50, 62, 86,
   90–91, 97
busing 132, 213–14

Caldwell, S. 76
Capper, C. 92, 97
career education 15
Carnegie 212
Carroll, J. 58, 66
Cawelti, G. 73, 81

Center on Organization and
    Restructuring of Schools
    169
centralization 69
Chan, C.K. 115
Chaos theory 18-21
charter schools 137–39, 141
Chavkin, N. 120, 121, 126
Chicago Public Schools
    69–70, 122
child benefit theory 133
China 5–6
choice 8, **127–45,** 149, 155
Chubb, J. 131, 136, 144
citizenship 216–17
Clark, R. 187–88, 189, 190,
    191
Coalition of Essential
    Schools 209
*Cochran vs. Louisiana State
    Board of Education* 133
compact disks 180, 183
competency based
    education 30, 55
competition 131, 142, 200
computers 183, 188–89
Conant, J. 212–13, 223
Cooperative Integrated
    Reading and
    Composition (CIRC) 198
cooperative learning 16, 21,
    35, 45, 122, 149, **193–06,**
    211
Cooperative learning Center
    195
Copernican plan 154
core blocks 154
Cotton, K. 72, 79, 80, 81,
    121, 124, 125, 152, 157,
    160, 189, 191

Crawford, D. 90, 95, 97
Crichton, M. 18
Cronin, J. 168, 175

Deal, T. 67
Demming, W.E. 85–91, 94,
    97
departmentalized schools
    154
Deutsch, M. 198, 202, 204
Dewey, J. 51, 62, 156,
Dumpty, H. 23
Dutch Freedom of
    Education Act 133

Educational Productivity
    Theory 124
effective schooling research
    125, 159
Eisner, E. 62
Elam, S. 143, 144
Ellis, A. 42, 50, 171, 175, 223
environments 17–18, 32, 34,
    215
Epstein, J. 117, 118

Farnan, P. 137–38, 144
Feuer, M. 172
Flesch, R. 211, 224
Food and Drug
    Administration (FDA)
    47
Ford, B. 157, 160
Fouts, J. 42, 50, 223
Friedman, M. 131
Fulton, K. 172

Gandara, P. 105, 109
Garnder, H. 43, 50
Gates, S. 63, 66
Gatto, J. 225
General Motors 7
Glasser, W. 87, 97, 98
Glazier, N. 144
Glenn, A. 185
Glickman, C.D. 10, 12
Good, T. 41
Goodlad, J.I. 6, 12, 41, 117,
     125, 137, 145, 152, 156,
     160, 187, 195, 205, 212,
     214, 215, 224
grading 163, 168
Guitierrez, R. 157, 160
Guskey, T. 63, 66

Habermas, J 30, 38, 114, 196,
     205
Haertel, G. 124, 126
Hallinan, M. 158, 160
Hannafin, R. 177, 184, 191
Harrison, C. 73, 81
Hawthorne effect 189
heterogeneous grouping
     153, 155
Heyns, B. 115, 125
higher education 133
Hoffer, E. 207
Hogland, R. 90, 95, 97
Holland (Netherlands) 77,
     133
Holt, M. 83, 85, 90–91, 98
home schools 130, 137

industrial psychology 7
industry 22, 85

information highway 185,
     218
innovations 16
instruction decisionmaking
     57
instructional groups **147–61**
instructional television
     179-180
interdisciplinary (integrat-
     ed) curriculum 30, 34,
     35, 149, 216–17
ITIP 30, 45

Jackson, P. 195, 205
Jamison, M. 92, 97
jigsaw 198–99
Johnson, D. 16, 41, 193, 197,
     199, 205
Johnson, R. 16, 41, 193, 197,
     199, 205, 207
Jolson, A. 184
Joplin plan 150–51, 155

Kagan, S. 198
Killion, J. 73, 81
Kliebard, H 69, 81
Kozma, R. 187–88, 189, 191
Kozol, J 127, 136, 145
Kuhn, T. 214, 224
Kulik, C. 63, 66, 147, 158,
     160, 189, 191
Kulik, J. 63, 66, 147, 158,
     160, 189, 191

Lange, J. 73, 75, 81
Lao, T. 222

Learning Together model
   197, 199
Lehman, N. 167, 175
Lewin, K. 201, 205
Liao, Y. 189, 191
Likert, R. 78, 95, 98
*List of Leading Cultural
   Indicators* 123
local control 69, 77
local school councils 69–70,
   122

Mager, R. 62
magnet schools 137, 139,
   154
Mann, H. 4, 131
mastery learning 15, 54–55,
   63
McClelland, D. 167
McGregor, D. 78, 81, 86, 95,
   98
McGurk, E. 157, 160
McKernan, J. 51, 62, 66
McLaughlin, M. 159, 160
McNeil, B. 189, 191
Melvin, C. 91, 98
Mencken, H.L. 210
Miller, B. 155, 157, 160, 161
Mitchell, J. 73, 81
Moe, T. 131, 136, 144
Montesorri, M. 156
Montgomery, M. 143
Mueller vs. Allen 130
Mulholland, L. 140–41, 145
multiage grouping—*see*
   nongraded education
multicultural education 122
multimedia 181, 183, 188
Mumford, L. 215

Murphy, C. 55, 66
Mussatti, D. 103

Nation At Risk 6, 12, 107
National Defense Education
   Act (NDEA) 212
National Education
   Association 3
National Goals for
   America's Schools 58
National Governors
   Association 9
National Governors
   Association 9
neighborhood schools 137,
   139
Nelson, K. 189, 191
New Math 15, 46, 87, 212
New Science 15, 87, 212
Newmann, F. 169, 176
Niemiec, R. 189, 191
Noddings, N. 41
nongraded education
   151–52, 155–58, 201, 211
Nongraded Elementary School
   152

O'Neil, J. 9, 11, 12, 13
occupational clusters 154
organizational theories
   77–78
Outcome Based Education
   7, 15, 21, **51–65,** 83,
   90–91, 94
Owens, R. 77, 81, 94, 98

P.L. 94–142 71

paideia 113
Pappert, S. 181, 191
parental involvement
    111–26
Pattern A and Pattern B
    leaders 78, 95
Pattison, M. 39
Pavan, B. 157, 161
Pearson, D. 41
Peltier, G. 99, 107, 109
performance assessment 172
Peterson, D. 79, 81
Piaget, J. 43, 50, 156, 195,
    205
Pigott, T. 63, 66
Pimentle, J. 157, 160
Place Called School 6, 12
*Politics, Markets, and
    America's Schools* 136
portfolios 32, 171–72
positive interdependence
    198
Pratt, D. 157, 161
private schools 129, 137, 140

Rankin, S. 87, 90, 98
Rasberry, 102, 107, 109
Rayborn, R. 174, 176
Raywid, A. 207
reductionism 62
Reform 6
Reich, R. 186
research
    applied (experimental)
        or Level 2 16,
        43, 47–48
    basic or Level 1 43, 48
    definitions of, **39–49**
    ex post facto 143

program evaluation or
    Level 3 29, 46, 48
qualitative 65
Restructuring
    arbitrary/mandated
        26–27, 30–33, 220–21
    authentic/fundamental
        33–37, 220–21
    bureaucratic/centralized
        33–37, 220–21
    components of 10
    definition of 6–11
    goal-driven/participa-
        tory 26–30, 220–21
Rioux, W. 111, 117, 119, 126
Roblyer, M. 189, 191
Russell, B. 23
Russia 5–6, 214
Ryan, A. 189, 192

Sarason, S. 209, 224
Sautter, R.140, 145
Savage Inequalities 136
Savenye, W. 177, 184, 191
Schaeffer, W. 127
scheduling 36
Schmoker, M. 95, 98
school calendars 8
school funding 71
schools within schools 29,
    137, 139, 154, 201, 212,
    217, 222–23
Shanker, A. 132
Sharan, S. 16
Sharan, S. 198, 199
Short, P. 41
Shulman, L. 41
Sinclair, U. 127

site-based management 21,
    34, **67–82**, 211
Sizer, T. 147, 209, 224
Slavin, R. 16, 41, 63, 66, 147,
    157, 158, 161, 193, 196,
    198–203, 205
social reconstructionist 92,
    123
Socrates 202
Spady, W. 51, 53–54, 59, 62,
    65–66
Spear, R. 147
Sputnik 211
Stallings, J. 63, 66
standardized tests 166–68,
    171
Stark, R. 125
Stevenson, H. 116, 126
Stipek, D. 63, 66
Strate, J. 127, 138, 143–44,
    145
Student Team Learning
    198–99
success principle 58
Sztajin, P. 92, 98, 143

Talbert, J. 159, 160
Taylor, F.W. 62, 85
Team Assisted Individual-
    ization (TAI) 197, 199
technology 17, 32, **177–92,**
    201, 211, 218
test scores 21
textbooks 20
Theory X and Theory Y 78,
    86, 95
Toch, T. 166, 176
Toffler, A. 17, 22
Total Quality Management

    8, **83–98**, 211
tracking 156
tuition tax credits, 130–31,
    137–38
Tyler, R. 62

United States Department
    of Education 12
USSR 212–13

Values clarification 15
violence, 20
virtual reality 187
vouchers 130–31, 134,
    137–38
Vygotsky, L. 195, 205

Walberg, H. 41, 58, 63, 66,
    124, 126, 189, 191
Wang, M. 124, 126
Wehlage, G. 169, 175
Weinstein, T. 189, 191
White, W. 105, 109
whole language 30, 32, 95,
    122, 201
Wiggins, G. 163
Wikelund, K. 121, 124, 125
Williams, D. 120. 121, 126
Wilson, C. 127, 138, 143–44,
    145
Wilson, R. 95, 98
Wingo, G. 209–10, 224
Wise, A. 13
Wood, F. 76
Worthen, B. 163, 171,
    173–74, 176

Year-Round Schools **99–109**
Young, R. 76, 81, 114, 126